Praise for
The Gospel You've Never Heard

"In his book, *The Gospel You've Never Heard*, Maurie Daigneau helps us see beyond words about the gospel, the 'good news' of Jesus, to the meaning of the gospel as it applies to our moment-by-moment living. Is it possible that many of us who claim to belong to Jesus are not truly following Jesus, in His way and on His terms? This author goes deeper with Jesus than most writers do. I'm thankful for that. I needed this book."

Roger C. Palms
Former editor of *Decision* magazine and author of fourteen books, including *God Guides Your Tomorrows*

"This is one of those rare books that address the spiritual crisis plaguing the United States of America, a world where right and wrong are no longer objective, but relative, where morality is no longer grounded on spiritual principles but personal interests. While the author bemoans the hypocrisy that he has witnessed in Christians, he writes with a voice filled with compassion and reassuring, engaging readers with questions that will push them to seek beyond the literal understanding of God's word in order to discover the hidden import of the Gospel."

A five-star review from **Romuald Dzemo**
Reviewer for Readers' Favorite®

"It was 1971, and a most memorable fall Saturday afternoon at Northwestern University's Ryan Field. I was watching my friend and quarterback Maurie Daigneau repeatedly pinpointing his receivers, completing pass after pass. 'Precise' was the only word that could describe Maurie's performance that afternoon, beating our Minnesota Gophers by a wide margin. Now, nearly fifty years later, Maurie has once again applied his precision skills to gain a more accurate understanding of the 'good news' to help all of us live by faith and understand how we can accede to 'take on' the mind of Christ."

Doug Kingsriter
Former NFL player, publisher,
and author of children's books and musicals

"Great writing. Great personal voice. I'm genuinely excited to see how Maurie is interacting with perspectives other than his own with clarity and grace, allowing their ideas to stand on their own. He is simply presenting his perspective and letting readers make up their minds."

Ed Cyzewski
Author of *Reconnect: Spiritual
Restoration from Digital Distraction*

"This work by Maurie Daigneau is a powerful personal polemic against 'easy believism' and a lack of understanding of the biblical gospel, logically presented and scripturally defended. The gospel is more than mere words. It is a gracious work that a triune God works in a person characterized by obedience. As Maurie clearly reveals, the making of a follower of Christ is the creation of a duplicate."

Dr. R. Bruce Bickel
Founder and president of the Transformational Leadership Group

"The book's approachable writing style blends experiences from the author's personal life [...] with astute analysis of Christian philosophy and the Bible, including the New Testament's original Greek. [...] This book is designed for personal reflection as well as group study, and the author concludes each chapter with a 'Deliberations' section that assigns additional research and asks probing questions. [...] An accessible and learned approach to Christianity."

—*Kirkus Reviews*

"In the twenty-first century, an emphasis on 'eternal security' has replaced an invitation to a breathtaking life of holy obedience in the Spirit. We need to be reminded that the Lord Jesus is able to express His resurrected life through the believer such that he will attain eternal life. This book is for all who desire genuine change into the sanctifying life of Christ. It is a call to wholeheartedly obey the Lord Jesus."

Fr. David Masterson
Founder of Gaudete Ministries

"In a time of declining global Christianity, Maurie Daigneau presents clarity and truth not seen in contemporary Christian writing. Maurie's life has been dedicated to the constant pursuit of a full and complete understanding of God's plan. His conclusions are based on countless hours of study and prayer in solitude, church, study groups, and seminary. Thankfully, he has chosen to share the truth with us."

Michael Maroney
President and CEO of Luxury to Legacy, LLC

The Gospel You've Never Heard

AN UNDERSTANDING THAT WILL
CHANGE YOUR LIFE

Maurie Daigneau

TRILOGY CHRISTIAN PUBLISHERS
TUSTIN, CA

Trilogy Christian Publishers
A Wholly Owned Subsidiary of Trinity Broadcasting Network
2442 Michelle Drive
Tustin, CA 92780

Copyright © 2021 by Maurie Daigneau

Cover design by Erika Alyana at erika.alyana@gmail.com

All scripture quotations are taken from the New American Standard Bible® (NASB), Copyright © 1960, 1962, 1963, 1968, 1971, 1972, 1973, 1975, 1977 by The Lockman Foundation. Used by permission. www.Lockman.org.

No part of this book may be reproduced, stored in a retrieval system, or transmitted by any means without written permission from the author.

All rights reserved, including the right to reproduce this book or portions thereof in any form whatsoever.

For information, address Trilogy Christian Publishing

Rights Department, 2442 Michelle Drive, Tustin, Ca 92780.

Trilogy Christian Publishing/ TBN and colophon are trademarks of Trinity Broadcasting Network.

For information about special discounts for bulk purchases, please contact Trilogy Christian Publishing.

Trilogy Disclaimer: The views and content expressed in this book are those of the author and may not necessarily reflect the views and doctrine of Trilogy Christian Publishing or the Trinity Broadcasting Network.

10 9 8 7 6 5 4 3 2 1

Library of Congress Cataloging-in-Publication Data is available.

ISBN 978-1-63769-344-5

ISBN 978-1-63769-345-2 (ebook)

To

Five by birth, now nine by marriage: Becky and Peter, Jenny and Charlie, Margaret, John and Ashley, and Laura and Ray, you are the arrows that fill my quiver beyond the fullest measure of joy and happiness. The steadfastness of your spirits and your commitments to godly living—and the thirteen grandchildren you have blessed us with—inspired me throughout the writing of this book.

Friday Morning Group.
Bruce, Dan, David, Doug, Jeff, Marty, Richie, Roland, Tim, and Troy, this book would not exist, but for the wisdom and encouragement you have shared with me throughout our years together. It is my sincerest hope that you will each recognize and hear a little bit of yourselves in what you read. You are my dearest brothers in Christ.

The Hard Workers.
Without the editing and review skills of Roger Psalms, Andi Cumbo-Floyd, Ed Cyzewski, Keith Carroll, and Professor Darrell Bock, this book would have never been worthy of a printed page. And a special thank you to Joel and Laura Pitney of Launch My Book, Inc. They held my hand throughout the entire publishing process, and I am most grateful for the guidance they provided.

The Invaluable.
My middle daughter Margaret is a professional educator by trade. She is the best teacher/communicator I know. Having her by my side was like having another version of myself, only smarter. The polish she added to the writing was invaluable. I trusted her communication skills implicitly. It was a good decision. Thanks, Marg!

The Indispensable.
Lastly, and without measure, my dearest Suse. Her everyday manner of living affirms how she loves the purpose of her life. She is the brightest and most constant light of the Lord in my life. This has, indeed, been the work of two as one.

Contents

Preface...xi

Introduction xiv

1. Times of Ignorance 1

2. The Concealed Now Revealed........................14

3. Appropriate Background Knowledge........... 26

4. Thread of Truth... 43

5. Beyond Confusion 54

6. Universal Inheritance................................... 66

7. Realizing Our Obligation 87

8. The Law Speaks... 104

9. No More Condemnation 124

10. Requirement of the Law.............................136

11. Relationship of Oneness 157

12. What About Eternal Life? 170

13. The Big Picture 189

14. The Bigger Picture...................................... 201

15. How Should We Live? 217

16. For Your Consideration 234

Endnotes 239

About the Author 246

The beginning of wisdom is: Acquire wisdom;
And with all your acquiring, get understanding.

Proverbs 4:7

Preface

The year was 1987. I was sixteen years into my faith-life journey. I was thirty-seven years old, a husband, a father, a business owner, and a very disillusioned Christian. I was nearing spiritual exhaustion and concerned about my ability to maintain the Christian façade. Hypocrisy had always been a troubling characteristic to me, especially when I saw it in the mirror.

I could no longer deny the obvious. My life experience was a far cry from contentment in any and every circumstance. Considering it all joy in the midst of the difficulties of life was not within my grasp. And to accept that all things happen for good to those who love God was simply a bridge too far. Does this sound familiar?

There were times during those days when I simply wanted to be left alone. But then I came across a book entitled *The Naked Church*. The subtitle read as follows: *Are you confused? Burned out? Devastated by the state of the church?* I had immediate answers to each of those questions. They were, respectively: "completely;" "not yet, but getting there;" and "without question!" The book was filled with anecdotes, quotes, and viewpoints that resonated deeply within my psyche.

I read and reread that book. It eventually led me into a deeper study of the Bible, where I arrived at this verse from Isaiah 5:13a: "Therefore, My people go into exile for their lack of knowledge." I researched the verse in the original Hebrew and learned that the word for "exile" is *galah*, which actually means "to be or to make naked." Thus, "My people are shown to be naked for their lack of knowledge."

Bingo! My frustration had something to do with a lack of knowledge. But how could that be? Aren't preachers around the world proclaiming the truth every Sunday? Aren't the world's libraries full of books that contain all there is to know about Christianity? Presumably, yes, and yes.

I continued to search and eventually came to the realization that the problem was more about a lack of understanding than it was a lack of knowledge. Perhaps in our haste, we, Christians, had missed the point of the proverb, "The beginning of wisdom is: Acquire wisdom; and with all your acquiring, *get understanding*" (Proverbs 4:7; emphasis mine).

I've always been passionate about things being "right." I'm a "fixer," a "straightener," and, most definitely, an "always read the directions first" kind of guy. I was feeling the prompting of the Lord, and I confess there were times when I wanted it to stop. I'm now

THE GOSPEL YOU'VE NEVER HEARD

grateful that it never did. I finally realized that it was time to be responsive to what I was hearing. I knew it was time to push the pause button.

The Lord kept affirming to me the benefit of being in His word. It took me a while to fully understand His meaning, but I eventually started to realize the need to begin spending my days at the feet of the only One I should have ever regarded as my Teacher.

With my wife's approval, I sold my business of fifteen years and rented a small office about a mile from the house. With a greater consistency than ever before, I began to hide His word in my heart. And as I did, I began to hear and learn as never before.

This book is about the result of that decision: the gaining of a gospel understanding that changed my life. I am now able to experience with a greater consistency the greatest desire of my heart: to be living my life in the same manner that our Lord lived His. It is my sincerest hope that this book might help you experience the same thing.

Introduction

After over fifty years as a believer, I would love to write a book about the increasingly beneficial impact that Christianity is having in America. But, unfortunately, it cannot be so. The Internet provides endless stories that present readily available evidence to the contrary. Go ahead and search "the decline of Christianity in America" or "hypocrisy in today's church" or, more heartbreakingly, "pastor sex scandal," and you will get my point.

If we are honest with ourselves, and, more importantly, with the One whom we claim to be following, we must admit what the evidence shows: we are falling short of the glory of God. If Jesus is truly living within us, it isn't always evident. It is hard to argue with the non-church world when they criticize what they are witnessing in the lives of Christians around them.

My purpose for writing this book is to delve into the reason for such a discrepancy and advance a perspective that the late Dallas Willard put forward in his book,

THE GOSPEL YOU'VE NEVER HEARD

The Divine Conspiracy: Rediscovering Our Hidden Life in God. He wrote:

> The most telling thing about the contemporary Christian is that he or she simply has no compelling sense that understanding of and conformity with the clear teachings of Christ is of any vital importance to his or her life, and certainly not that it is in any way essential [...] More than any other single thing, in any case, *the practical irrelevance of actual obedience to Christ* accounts for the weakened effect of Christianity in the world today.[1]

I believe the principal reason for this "practical irrelevance" was succinctly captured by a popular author and leading pastor when, a little more than a decade ago, he declared: "I don't think we've got the gospel right yet..."[2] I agree with that sentiment, and this book tells why. I did not write *The Gospel You've Never Heard* to intentionally repeat anything. I wrote it to clarify and bring to light an understanding of the gospel that has been lost to the church and the world for a very long time. It needs to be rediscovered. That is what this book is about.

Additional Motivation

I also wrote this book because of my growing concerns for our country, our world, and my grandchil-

xv

dren. A little over four years ago, in an article entitled "Americans Worry About Moral Decline, Can't Agree on Right and Wrong," Scott McConnell, executive director of LifeWay Research, noted that there had been a huge shift between the way older (older than forty-five) and younger (thirty-five or younger) Americans think about morality. Stability regarding moral rights and wrongs is no longer the norm. He stated:

> We are shifting very fast from a world where right and wrong didn't change to a world where right and wrong are relative [...] We are not all on the same page when it comes to morality. And we haven't reckoned with what that means.[3]

What it means is the inevitability of exactly what we are now seeing in the United States: division, strife, violence, destruction, and hatred, all being fostered by a free-for-all rhetoric that is at levels we have not heard in quite some time. There is not a direction in which a finger is not pointed. However, my intention is not to belabor those realities. Instead, I offer a solution that is by no means original but by every means the only true remedy for our malady. I offer a clarification of the gospel of the Lord Jesus Christ.

Agreement is Needed

There is nothing of greater importance to the world than the proper understanding of God's gospel message. And there is nothing more devastating to the world than the failure of our most prestigious gospel preachers and teachers to agree on its meaning. As theologian Jackson Wu recently noted:

> In recent years countless books, articles, and blogs have debated the question, "What is the gospel?" [...] There seems to be as much diversity as there is agreement when defining what exactly is the gospel.[4]

It is as though we've missed the point of the apostle Paul's admonition to be "of the same mind with one another according to Christ Jesus; that with one accord [we] may with one voice glorify the God and Father of our Lord Jesus Christ" (Romans 15:5–6; hereinafter, comments in square brackets are mine).

The Bible says that "understanding is a fountain of life to him who has it" (Proverbs 16:22). Jesus promised that if we remained in His word, we could "know [and understand] the truth" (see John 8:31–32). Toward that end, I encourage you to have a Bible close by as you read and to expect the need to use it often. I would also encourage you to read this book more than once. It is meant to be challenging, thought-provoking, and quite possibly deeply convicting.

xvii

Gospel Terms and Phrases

You will notice a frequent use of the word "gospel." For clarification, it is not used as a specific reference to any of the first four books of the New Testament: Matthew, Mark, Luke, and John. It is used as a reference to what is often referred to as "good news." In Greek, the word for the "gospel message" is *euaggelion*, which implies a message of "good news."[5] This book is about the foundational specifics of that "good news" message.

There is nothing more important for an accurate understanding of the gospel than an accurate understanding of its frequently used terms and phrases. Here is just a partial listing of what you will encounter on these pages:

- the difference between "having faith" and "living by faith;"
- the difference between "full and exact" knowledge and "partial" knowledge;
- the message and reality of two salvations: one that is immediately completed and one that waits to be accomplished "in the last time;"
- the experience of "here and now" eternal life vs. one that can be realized only as a Judgment Day reward;
- a recognition of what it means to be in possession of the "mind of Christ;"

THE GOSPEL YOU'VE NEVER HEARD

- an understanding of the only two spiritual conditions in which human beings exist: regenerate and unregenerate;
- a vivid picture of what it means to have the Lord "driving your spiritual car;"
- an accurate understanding of the word "obligation" and to whom it applies;
- an understanding of the "here and now" twofold objective of the gospel and how that objective can be achieved;
- and, most of all, a recognition of the only One any of us are to call "Teacher."

As you continue through the pages of this book, it is my hope that the Lord opens your heart, challenges your mind, and speaks directly to your soul. Whatever your current level of faith, however solid your current foundation, it is my fervent prayer that this book and its message will forever change your life, your walk, and your day-to-day relationship with our Lord and Savior Jesus Christ.

1

Times of Ignorance

My original exposure to God was largely a result of my mom's wonderful voice. She was the lead soloist in the church choir, and every Sunday morning, my sister and I would find ourselves in a pew with instructions to behave or else. We very much enjoyed those Sunday mornings listening to our mother sing. In addition, from my earliest memory, I was always under the impression that this was the place where people met with God. As a result, I can't remember a time during the days of my youth when I considered anything contrary to the existence of God. I mean, how else could this incredible world have gotten here? There didn't seem to be any reason to doubt.

I was eventually baptized at the age of twelve and summarily congratulated for becoming a Christian. The task going forward, or so I was told, was to try every day to be a good person. How good? At least as good as the next person. So, for me, by definition, being a Christian meant just that: be a good person.

I'd like to think that being good was always my top priority. But from my earliest days, the great desire of my life was to become a good athlete. My parents were divorced when I was two, and my dad took off, leaving my mom to raise my sister and me by herself. She was a great encourager of my athletic talents from the moment I began to display them. Football, basketball, and baseball became my passions, and she was always my biggest fan.

By the time I reached high school, I was good enough to become all-conference in all three sports and eventually received a full scholarship to play football as a quarterback at Northwestern University (NU). As a graduating high school senior, I felt like I literally had the world by the tail. Good person, you kidding? Great athlete! How else could I have gotten where I was?

I'm Going Camping

Fast forward a bit. The summer of 1971 was approaching. I had just finished my junior year at NU. That fall (1970) was my first full season as the starting quarterback, and we'd gone 6–1 in conference play, finishing in second place in the Big Ten. We had just finished our spring practice season, and I was cleaning out my locker, thinking about heading home for the summer. An assistant coach got my attention and motioned for me to follow him to his office. In a matter of minutes, I was talking on the phone with some guy from an organization called the Fellowship of Christian Athletes (FCA).

THE GOSPEL YOU'VE NEVER HEARD

I hung up the phone and looked at Coach Lile. He was sitting across from me with a big grin on his face. "Have a great time," he said.

A few weeks later, I was getting out of a car in the middle of the mountains in Estes Park, Colorado. I'd arrived at a place called the YMCA of the Rockies. I was going to be spending a week at my first-ever FCA camp. I was nervous, to say the least, but comforted by the fact that there were other college athletes in attendance, as well as a handful of NFL players. The NFL players were going to be the speakers for the week, and we, college guys, were going to be individually responsible for leading small groups of high school athletes. It was going to be a week of what they called "perspiration and inspiration."

As far as I was concerned, the perspiration part was no problem. The inspiration was another story. I'd rather have been standing across from an Ohio State linebacker than sitting in a circle (actually called a huddle) with a bunch of high school athletes, trying to teach them about what it meant to be a Christian.

But then something very real started to happen. On that very first day, I began sensing something, mostly in and through the presence of others. I heard words from guys like Willie Lanier, Jerry Mays, and Jerry Stovall, all NFL players, and also from Doug Kingsriter, a great tight end from the University of Minnesota. They were words that suggested that perhaps my definition of

3

what it meant to be a Christian was a little lacking, a little shallow.

There was consistency in what they said. It was about a relationship: a relationship that, for them, was the most important relationship they had in their lives. I knew it was a relationship that I did not have. It was one thing to believe in the existence of God but something entirely different to have surrendered my life to the Lord Jesus Christ.

The ensuing time was full of discussions and continuing personal interactions. But on the early morning of the third day, I found myself in a circle with about six or seven other guys. We were kneeling and holding hands. The tight end from Minnesota was in the circle. It had become obvious to me that he had the relationship I was looking for, the presence that I had sensed almost from the moment of my arrival at the camp.

It also occurred to me that without an invitation, the Lord Jesus was not going to presumptively take up residence in my life (see Revelation 3:20). I knew I had never previously extended Him such an invitation. I prayed from the depths of my heart for His presence to become mine. The Spirit of the Lord had arrived in my life, and I knew it was for the very first time.

An Unshakeable Relationship

It has been fifty years since that moment in Colorado, that moment when my faith-life journey really began. A lot has happened in the days and years that have followed: joys and sorrows, victories and defeats, right and wrong choices, trials and tribulations, certainties and doubts. But there is one thing that I have never been able to shake, though the Lord knows there were times when I tried.

No matter how difficult the circumstances of my life, no matter what anybody said about my faith, about the book that I followed, about the Savior that I believed in, no matter what evidence they presented to deny the truth of what I believed, what could not be done, what could not be denied, what could not be taken from me, was the reality of the presence of the One who had entered my life in that moment in the mountains of Colorado.

That is the unshakable reality that has led to the writing of this book. If I have learned anything over the course of the years of my relationship with the Lord, it is the measure of the incredible patience He has for anyone who is sincerely seeking to know Him and His truth.

Through the many times I was stumbling around, looking in all the wrong places, listening to all the wrong voices, He patiently waited for me to finally discover the only place that He and I could ever truly meet. "If you abide in My word, *then* you are truly disciples of Mine; and you shall know the truth, and the truth shall make you free" (John 8:31b–32).

Answers from My Own Quest

Any and every faith perspective regarding Christianity emanates from the same source, the Bible. Without it, there would be no Christian faith to discuss. The knowledge the Bible contains is essential to the discussion if one hopes to find and understand the true meaning and purpose of life.

The difficulty in today's world is that the credibility of the Bible hangs by a thread if it has any at all. In his book *Letter to a Christian Nation*, noted atheist/author Sam Harris suggested that it is long past time to "admit that the Bible is merely a collection of imperfect books written by highly fallible human beings."[1]

And similarly, in his book *god is not Great*, fellow atheist/author (the late) Christopher Hitchens wrote:

> The case for biblical consistency or authenticity or "inspiration" has been in tatters for some time, and the rents and tears only become more obvious with better research, and thus no "revelation" can be derived from that quarter.[2]

Of course, criticism from the nonbelieving community is to be expected, but when a world-class biblical scholar, Bart D. Erhman, abandons his evangelical view of the inerrancy and divine inspiration of the Bible, what are we to think? The mere title of one of his many books, *Jesus, Interrupted: Revealing the Hidden Contradic-*

THE GOSPEL YOU'VE NEVER HEARD

tions in the Bible (and Why We Don't Know About Them), tells me a lot about his perspective.

However, unlike Harris and Hitchens, and in spite of the fact that he now sees the Bible as nothing more or less than a "very human book,"[3] at least Erhman continues to encourage that we "read, study and cherish the Bible."[4] Thank you, Mr. Erhman!

The Bible—My Primary Source

If the above weren't enough to muddy the biblical waters, there are a growing number of voices within the church itself that are acknowledging the obvious: "biblical literacy in America is at an all-time low."[5] Of course, the awareness of declining biblical literacy is not a new reality; it is something that has been trending for decades.

In 2009, George Barna (The Barna Group) noted from his research that:

> There is shockingly little growth evident in people's understanding of the fundamental themes of the scriptures and amazingly little interest in deepening their knowledge and application of biblical principles.[6]

In 1990, George Gallup and Jim Castelli concluded, "Americans revere the Bible, but, by and large, they don't read it. And because they don't read it, they have become a nation of biblical illiterates."[7] And if we look back even further, the witness of J. C. Ryle's classic work, *Holiness*, originally written in 1877, was this:

> There is an amazing ignorance of scripture among many and the consequent want of established solid religion. In no other way can I account for the ease with which people are like children, tossed to and fro, and carried about by every wind of doctrine.[8]

I reference the above perspectives because, despite its critics and the illiteracy issues, the Bible must and will be the primary source for my writing. As such, I think it important for readers to know that my convictions regarding the book are not complicated. I hold to the belief that one day I will be required to give an account for the way I chose to live my life.

For such an important moment of accountability to be just, it presumes the application of a standard of measure that I could have and, therefore, should have known during my lifetime. Since the Bible has always been available to me (albeit clearly not the case for everyone), I believe that in that moment, were I to ask the Lord Jesus how it was that I should have known and understood the standard by which He would be judging me, He might respond to me as follows:

THE GOSPEL YOU'VE NEVER HEARD

"For the LORD gives wisdom; from His mouth *come* knowledge and understanding."

Proverbs 2:6

"It is written, 'MAN SHALL NOT LIVE ON BREAD ALONE, BUT ON EVERY WORD THAT PROCEEDS OUT OF THE MOUTH OF GOD.'"

Matthew 4:4

"If any man is willing to do His will, he shall know of the teaching."

John 7:17a

"If you abide in My word, *then* you are truly disciples of Mine; and you shall know the truth, and the truth shall make you free."

John 8:31b–32

I am convinced that God not only inspired this "very human book" but also protected a thread of unbroken truth that runs through the Bible, all the way from the first word in Genesis to the last word in Revelation. Despite the historical-critical shortcomings that "better research" has revealed, I believe it to be the only completely reliable source in which I can find the "WORD THAT PROCEEDS OUT OF THE MOUTH OF GOD" (Matthew 4:4).

A person's ability to know and understand the promised truth that will make him or her free depends upon

9

the way he or she seeks to know and understand the truth that the Bible contains. And it is a truth that we should not be leaving in the hands of someone else to figure out. We should be seeking to know it ourselves because it can be known. There is simply no better book to be seeking to understand as we endeavor to make sense out of the meaning and purpose of our lives.

In the concluding chapter of his aforementioned book, Christopher Hitchens quotes German philosopher Gotthold Lessing's response to Lutheran pastor/theologian Johann Goeze during the latter's unsuccessful four-year (1777–1781) attempt to convert Lessing to Christianity. Hitchens cites the following from Lessing:

> The true value of a man is not determined by his possession, supposed or real, of Truth, but rather by his sincere exertion to get to the Truth. It is not possession of the Truth, but rather the pursuit of Truth by which he extends his powers and in which his ever-growing perfectibility is to be found. Possession makes one passive, indolent, and proud. If God were to hold all Truth concealed in his right hand, and in his left only the steady and diligent drive for Truth, albeit with the proviso that I would always and forever err in the process, and to offer me the choice, I would with all humility take the left hand.[9]

The choice that Mr. Lessing (and the late Mr. Hitchens) is affirming, the preferred choice of the left hand, is a choice made by far too many throughout the course of human history. Intentionally or otherwise, that choice avoids the personal accountability that comes with knowing what God was concealing in His right hand.

The irony is He no longer conceals anything in His right hand. The truth of all that matters was revealed some two thousand years ago through the life of Jesus Christ. And you do not need to be a rocket scientist or a degreed theologian to know and understand it; you just have to desire the knowing and the understanding "with all your heart" (Jeremiah 29:13b).

A Magnificent Oratory

There is a story in the Bible (see Acts 17:16–34) that tells of a time when the apostle Paul was called upon to deliver a speech regarding what his requesters considered to be "some strange things to [their] ears" (v. 20a). They had overheard him preaching these "strange things" while in the marketplace in the ancient city of Athens, Greece.

The place for the presentation was called the Areopagus. It was where philosophers, faith-practitioners, and truth-seekers from throughout the ancient world would regularly gather to discuss and debate their various philosophical and religious perspectives. They were always seeking answers and, whenever the opportunity presented itself, were especially interested in hearing about new teachings.

Paul's message was artfully diplomatic yet piercingly declaratory. After commending their religiosity, he made it very clear that they need not continue their worship of "AN UNKNOWN GOD" (Acts 17:23). "We ought not to think," he said, "that the Divine Nature is like gold or silver or stone, an image formed by the art and thought of man" (v. 29). Such thinking, he went on to say, belonged to "the times of ignorance," times that God had previously "overlooked" (v. 30a).

With a speech that has proven ageless for its significance, Paul was not condemning what had been their natural effort; he was simply declaring that what they sought to find in ignorance they could now know as revealed truth. The God by whom "we live and move and exist" (v. 28a) was:

> Now declaring to men that all everywhere should repent, because He has fixed a day in which He will judge the world in righteousness through a Man whom He has appointed, having furnished proof to all men by raising Him from the dead.
>
> **Acts 17: 30b–31**

All in all, it is a rather remarkable declaration from a man who had previously been a persecutor of anyone who had claimed allegiance to this God-appointed Man (see Galatians 1:13). This book has been written with an eye toward that "fixed day," in the hope that we might all be better prepared when it arrives because it will arrive!

THE GOSPEL YOU'VE NEVER HEARD

Deliberations
Questions for Reflection or Group Study

1. What are the origins of your faith? By whom were you taught? Journal or discuss what you believe and why you believe it.
2. Read John 8:31–32 and consider the following:
   - True disciples of the Lord are people who do what?
   - Where does meaningful engagement with the Bible stand as a priority in your life?
   - What are some of the inhibitors to the frequency of personal time spent studying Scripture, and how might they be overcome?
   - What is the promised outcome?
3. Contemplate the significance of Paul's Areopagus message (Acts 17: 22–31). Summarize what you believe to be the key points of his message.

2

The Concealed Now Revealed

Sam Harris writes that the time has come to acknowledge that "theology is now little more than a branch of human ignorance. Indeed, it is ignorance with wings."[1] According to the apostle Paul, Mr. Harris's viewpoint was once correct. But the fact is that such a time was two thousand years ago. For it was then that "the times of ignorance" (Acts 17:30a) were wonderfully and miraculously ended.

On more than one occasion, in his later writings, Paul would refer to his message as a message of the revelation of the "manifold wisdom of God" (Ephesians 3:10a), the wisdom that had previously been a long-kept secret. By the intention of God, it had been hidden from the past ages and generations in a mystery that was not to be revealed until the coming of Christ (see Romans 16:25b; Colossians 1:26a). But this wisdom was now being made known by Paul and the other disciples in "the

THE GOSPEL YOU'VE NEVER HEARD

preaching of Jesus Christ" (Romans 16:25a). It was a preaching that was intended to lead to a "full assurance of understanding, *resulting* in a true knowledge of God's mystery, *that is*, Christ *Himself*, in whom are hidden all the treasures of wisdom and knowledge" (Colossians 2:2b–3).

So why then do so many people believe and live as though the essence of truth is simply something that cannot be known with any degree of certainty? Or worse yet, that the truth is something that we are entirely free to author on our own, without any resulting consequence. In his last letter, Paul wrote that a time would come:

> When they will not endure sound doctrine, but *wanting* to have their ears tickled, they will accumulate for themselves teachers in accordance to their own desires; and will turn away their ears from the truth, and will turn aside to myths.
>
> **2 Timothy 4:3–4**

It is my conviction that the true knowledge of God's mystery, that is, the true knowledge of Christ Himself, though clearly revealed in the Bible, has been replaced with a doctrine designed to tickle the ear, a doctrine that has prevented people from knowing the truth as God intended it to be known and understood.

In his book *The End of Faith*, Sam Harris makes the following observation:

We believe most of what we believe about the world because others have told us to. Reliance upon the authority of experts, and upon the testimony of ordinary people, is the stuff of which worldviews are made [...] There are good arguments and bad ones, precise observations and imprecise ones; and each of us has to be the final judge of whether or not it is reasonable to adopt a given belief about the world.[2]

I quite agree with Mr. Harris's observation, and to his point, the Bible affirms that "as [a man] thinks within himself, so he is" (Proverbs 23:7a). If this is true, I should be mindful of the things I believe and why I believe them. Am I a self-taught thinker, or have I relied on the teaching and instruction of someone else, perhaps my parents or my religious leaders, some theologian(s) from antiquity, or a contemporary with presumed good intentions and the proper academic credentials? Is the truth of God really just a matter of human opinion, nothing more or less than an ever-evolving product of the intellect of man?

A Disappointing Discovery

I have become convinced that the reason so many believe the mystery remains unsolved is not because they lack the ears to hear (see Matthew 11:15) but is rather a result of an unintentionally misplaced trust.

THE GOSPEL YOU'VE NEVER HEARD

Most people trust the leaders of their faith communities. They assume that what is being taught from the pulpit and in their community study groups is an accurate representation of biblical truth. My wife and I had just such an expectation when we joined our first evangelical church.

Within a couple of years, we were actively involved in a neighborhood group comprised of a dozen married couples ranging in age from early thirties to mid-fifties. A year or two later, I was elected to the governing body of the church as a representative of younger families. We were at peace and grateful for our growth and everything that was happening in our lives as we invested in our faith and church community.

I lasted barely a year on the governing board. I was expecting an experience of leadership in which the resolution of real and sometimes substantial church-life problems would be centered on seeking guidance from and finding unanimity in the Holy Spirit. Instead, I found ego and power and the need for personal control, the likes of which I had never seen in any secular board room. I was devastated.

At the same time, some of the marriages within our neighborhood group began to fail. Over the next few years, six of the twelve marriages would end in divorce, and another would be ended because the husband committed suicide. Something very troubling became obvious to my wife and me. Far too many people within the church were living no differently than people in the world. And their favorite mantra was: "We know we're not perfect, but at least we're forgiven!" Something was terribly wrong.

The Bible says that people who claim to know Christ ought to walk in the same manner as He walked (see 1 John 2:4–6). How could life in His church be so visibly and acceptably contrary? Why was the church so unwilling to measure the credibility of its profession by the substance of its performance? I began to struggle mightily with bitterness, anger, and an overwhelming anxiety such as I had never experienced before.

Confessing the Realities of My Struggles

One thing I have always appreciated about the world of athletics is that by its nature, it doesn't allow much room, if any, for hypocrisy. No matter what anyone said about his or her skills, abilities, and strengths, it was always their visible performance that gave substance to the verbal claims. There is no place to hide when one steps into the arena of competition. The level of our abilities becomes readily apparent. In contrast, the hypocrisy within the church was very visible and very troubling.

Then one day, it hit me. It mattered not what the church or any individual had or had not done; what mattered most was that I was failing the test of my faith (see 2 Corinthians 13:5). I was allowing the circumstances of my life to control my disposition. The bitterness was affecting my performance as a husband,

THE GOSPEL YOU'VE NEVER HEARD

as a father, and as a follower of Christ. This was a trial within which I could find no joy (see James 1:2). And in the moment, I felt as if there was nothing I could do about it.

I began to openly confess the realities of my struggles to the Lord, though I had no doubt He was aware of them. I knew the problem was not His, but mine. There was something I did not understand, something I was missing, but what was it? What would He have me do?

In one of those moments of searching, I recalled an experience I had as a young boy of ten or so. In those days, if I wasn't eating or sleeping or fidgeting in a classroom, I was playing with some kind of ball. In the fall, it was a football, in the winter, a basketball, and in the summer, a baseball. On many occasions, some of us would stay on the playground after school and play our sports until dinnertime approached and it was time to go home.

I lived a block and a half away from school and was generally the last one to leave. I often ended up being on the playground by myself. It was never a problem, though, for I always found a way to practice.

One afternoon I was alone with just my ball and glove and, as I had done so many times before, was throwing the ball up against the brick of the schoolhouse wall and fielding it as it bounced back to me. Sometimes easy, sometimes hard, sometimes to the left, and sometimes to the right: how many times could I toss it without a miss? Once when one got by me (not an infrequent oc-

19

currence in those days), and I turned to retrieve it, I saw Mr. Cheever, the school principal, bend down and swoop it up flawlessly. He walked over to me with a big grin on his face, ball in hand, and knelt to look me squarely in the eyes.

Mr. Cheever was a very special man to me. I was growing up without a father, and on many occasions, he would uniquely fill that void. No one did that more frequently or better for me than Mr. Cheever. He played sports with us every day during lunch and was always fair and honest. He always picked the teams impartially and made us learn to play with each other as teammates.

I knew Mr. Cheever loved me and wished only for my best as well as that of all the kids. When he spoke, I listened. "Maurie," he said, "I've been watching you here for several minutes, as I have on many occasions in the past, and I want to encourage you. If you remember to go at everything you do in life with as much dedication and passion as you do your sports, you'll be very successful."

In that moment of remembering, I felt the conviction of the Lord. I knew what it felt like to be intense, to focus, and to push myself to be the best athlete I could be. I also knew that I had never sought to know and understand the Lord or His word with that kind of intensity and devotion. The course I was to take from then on became obvious to me.

With my wife's blessing, I restructured my vocational life, entered into an agreement to divest my business interests, and began to work toward freeing up my days that I might begin to fully seek the Lord. It was the beginning of a journey that would eventually teach me that in this life, the most important possession any person can have is not just the knowledge of God but, more importantly, the understanding that goes with it.

The Only One I Call Teacher

Early on, I was somewhat uncertain of the study approach I should take. So much of what I believed at that point was just as Sam Harris had noted: it was the sum of what others had told me, of what I had gleaned from a casual reading of the Bible and the writings of others (books, commentaries, etc.). I eventually found a beginning direction from this verse in the Epistle of James: "But if any of you lacks wisdom, let him ask of God, who gives to all men generously and without reproach, and it will be given to him" (James 1:5). I knew it was time for me to seek the Lord through prayer, and I knew I needed to approach it differently than I had ever done before. It needed to be a conversation where I would not only speak but listen.

It was not by accident that a quick church library search found me in possession of a marvelous little writing entitled *A Treasury of Prayer* by Leonard Ravenhill. It lifted me in such a way that I found myself wondering if what I had been doing before was truly prayer. It was slow going at first because it took me a while to learn how to quiet my heart and to listen. But soon, I began to hear His voice…"There are two things you must do in your search for My truth. You must abide principally in My word, not the word of others; and, you must regard Me as your only Teacher."

From that moment forward, I determined to remain steadfast in my commitment to the teaching voice of the only One any of us is to call "Teacher" (see Matthew 23:8b). I maintained my use of concordances and lexicons to stay as true to the original biblical languages (Hebrew and Greek) as possible. But I resolved to leave my numerous and previously studied commentaries (interpretive opinions of others) on the shelf.

By drawing nearer to Him and His word, I have experienced Him drawing nearer to me (see James 4:8a), and in the process, I have become convinced that the Bible does contain the spiritual words that represent the spiritual thoughts that emanate from the mind of the very One before whom we will all one day stand (see 1 Corinthians 2:13b, 16b; Acts 17:31; Romans 2:5–11; Hebrews 9:27).

No More Pretending

It is my sincere belief that the foundational truths of the mystery made known (see Colossians 1:25–27) through the life, death, and resurrection of Jesus Christ are no longer being clearly presented (or agreed upon) by many in the modern church. As a result, the truth that was delivered "in all wisdom and insight [...] *that is,*

THE GOSPEL YOU'VE NEVER HEARD

the summing up of all things in Christ" (Ephesians 1:8b, 10a) is no longer widely known or rightly understood.

This is not to suggest that what is currently happening is being done intentionally. It is very true that much of what is currently being preached is what I believed for many years. But as I noted above, I finally reached a point when I could no longer deny the shallowness of my experience. I was done pretending for the sake of appearance. I was never more ready to learn.

This book presents the study by which my original understanding of those foundational truths, identified in a booklet called *The Four Spiritual Laws*[3], was changed considerably. What I now know to be true regarding the gospel of the Lord Jesus Christ is entirely different from what I first heard and embraced. I offer what I have learned as a means of encouragement and direction to anyone whose current faith-life experience is similar to what mine had been, anyone who believes that the essence of truth continues to remain beyond our understanding, and anyone simply searching for meaning and purpose in life.

By now, you have probably realized that this is not a two-hour airplane book. I offer it as a tool of instruction that will require some intentional brain time. I anticipate that for many of you, the source document and the cast of characters will seem familiar. But I am quite certain that the narrative being revealed will be considerably different from what many of you have previously known. And I repeat my earlier suggestion: having your

23

Bible close by will prove helpful. Yes, it may slow your journey through this book, but it will help to affirm the source of my writing and the identity of our Teacher.

With that in mind, I want to emphasize that I take very seriously the admonition that it would be "better for a millstone to be hung around [my] neck and [I] be thrown into the sea than for [me] to cause [anyone] to stumble" (see Matthew 18:6; Luke 17:2), and as such, I assume full responsibility for my conclusions. I do so because I accept what the Lord promised:

1. If we are willing to do His will, we will "know of the teaching" (John 7:17).
2. If we abide [remain] in His word, we will "know the truth" (John 8:31–32).
3. It will be by His Spirit that we will be guided into "all the truth" (John 16:13).

Though I believe very deeply in the truth of what I have written—largely because of the above promises—it should not be my work or beliefs that convince any person of anything. There is only One who can validate in each of our hearts the accuracy of what we read and, with all due respect, it is not a minister or priest, a rabbi or imam, or the latest best-selling author featured on *Super Soul Sunday*. Ultimately, it is God's word that filters all others. "For the LORD gives wisdom; from His mouth *come* knowledge and understanding" (Proverbs 2:6).

THE GOSPEL YOU'VE NEVER HEARD

Deliberations

Questions for Reflection or Group Study

1. What does the Bible say about the "truth of God"? Can it be known, or is it still "hidden in a mystery"?

2. What does scripture say about a person who claims to know the Lord but does not live in a manner that evidences the relationship (see 1 John 2:3–6)?

3. Read Jeremiah 29:13 and verbalize in your own words what you think it means. Regarding your knowledge of Jesus and His truth, can you relate to such a manner of seeking? What would it mean in your life if you recognized and regarded the Lord as the only one any of us are to call "Teacher"?

3

Appropriate Background Knowledge

Jesus referred to Himself as the "light of the world" (John 8:12), and it is my conviction that the gospel message, properly understood, serves as a prism, a clarifier of the true light (see John 1:9), through which the kind intention (see Ephesians 1:5, 9) of all God had purposed in His Son can be known and understood. Just as a prism clarifies the component colors of light, the proper understanding of the gospel makes known the truths of God. Such an understanding of the gospel is critical.

I did not have that understanding during the early years of my faith-life journey, and it is one that I now hold to dearly. I ask you to consider temporarily closing your current "Gospel Understanding" file and opening a new one. If you read something that presents an understanding that is different from the one you currently hold, save it in the new file. You will always be able to delete the new and reopen the old at any time. But before you do any deleting, I would simply encourage that you be like the Bereans, who steadfastly took whatever they were hearing to the Scriptures "to *see* whether these things were so" (Acts 17:11b).

The Communicator's Intended Meaning

Famed author and speaker Tony Robbins once said, "The way we communicate with ourselves and others ultimately determines the quality of our lives." Albert Einstein once said, "Any fool can know. The point is to understand." The gospel of the Lord Jesus Christ is the most important communication God has ever sent to His creation. It is critical that we know and understand the truth of that gospel as it was intended to be known and understood. Since it is the truth by which we will ultimately be judged, we must be certain that we understand the communication as intended by God, not as determined by the thought of man.

To highlight the key to the accurate understanding of any communication, I want to reference first a book called *Cultural Literacy: What Every American Needs to Know*. Written in 1987 by Professor E. D. Hirsch, Jr., of the University of Virginia, the book identifies what he believes to be the necessary prerequisite to the proper understanding of any form of communication.

His thesis statement, "Without appropriate background knowledge, people cannot adequately understand written or spoken language,"[1] was well substantiated throughout the book. A study he conducted, which

is involving the following paragraph, is extremely in-
formative. It reads:

> The procedure is quite simple. First, you arrange
> the items in different groups. Of course, one pile
> may be sufficient depending upon how much
> there is to do. If you have to go somewhere else
> due to a lack of facilities that is the next step. Oth-
> erwise you are pretty well set.[2]

Do you recognize and understand what the above
paragraph means? In the study, several groups were
given this paragraph to read, apart from any other
knowledge. Not one person in any of the groups could
recognize the sentences from the paragraph, except the
group that had, in addition to the paragraph, been giv-
en the title, "Washing Clothes." That title enabled the
readers to "integrate the sentences into a mental model that they constructed from prior knowledge about
washing clothes."[3] The model gave meaning to the sentences; thus, the intended communication of the paragraph could be properly understood.

Until such time as God chose to reveal the "appropriate background knowledge" through the gospel of
His Son (the "Washing Clothes" knowledge), the purpose and meaning of the first four thousand years
(biblical timeline estimate) of human history could
not be fully understood. This inability to understand is
the pre-Christ condition of all human beings that was

THE GOSPEL YOU'VE NEVER HEARD

referenced by Paul early in his Romans letter when he quoted from the psalmist, "THERE IS NONE RIGHTEOUS, NOT EVEN ONE; THERE IS NONE WHO UNDERSTANDS" (Romans 3:10–11a). This was the universal condition of the whole of humanity at the time because the Son of God had not yet brought understanding into the world (see 1 John 5:20a).

There is a second and equally significant point (not mentioned in Hirsch's book) that concerns the absolute necessity of properly interpreting that "Washing Clothes" knowledge of the gospel. Referring back to the thesis statement of his book, we note the word "appropriate." If a hearer is to discern a communicator's intended meaning accurately, he or she must be certain that the drawn upon background knowledge is the appropriate knowledge.

Reread Hirsch's "Washing Clothes" paragraph below. Only this time, do it from the perspective created by the title, "Filing Paperwork":

> The procedure is quite simple. First, you arrange the items in different groups. Of course, one pile may be sufficient depending upon how much there is to do. If you have to go somewhere else due to a lack of facilities that is the next step. Otherwise you are pretty well set.

Did you notice that this title also gives meaning to the paragraph? However, it is not the meaning intended by the communicator. Apart from the direct intervention of the communicator, or someone else who knows the true intent of the communication, the reader has no way of knowing that he or she has misunderstood the communication. The reader would assume his or her position of understanding to be in harmony with the intent of the communicator and proceed completely unaware that such an understanding was actually erroneous. Regarding the gospel, I believe this to be an unintentional reality of which many in today's church are unaware.

A Story to Foster Comprehension

As an additional means of fostering an accurate understanding of the "Washing Clothes" knowledge of the gospel, I've created an allegorical narrative. It is intended to serve as a framework narrative of a "bigger picture" (more on this in chapters "The Big Picture" and "The Bigger Picture") that will help you better understand the reading that lies ahead. You might think of it as the "appropriate background knowledge."

The narrative also serves as a beginning introduction to a very important gospel teaching. There are only two spiritual conditions in which human beings can exist: unregenerate and regenerate. Both will be explained in greater detail later in the book.

The Bible tells us that "the LORD God formed man of the dust from the ground, and breathed into his nostrils the breath of life; and man became a living being"

THE GOSPEL YOU'VE NEVER HEARD

(Genesis 2:7). Think of yourself as that first created person at the very beginning of the journey of human life. Your body is the vehicle for this journey. Think of it as a car crafted from the dust of the ground, with your God-breathed soul as its only passenger. Your hands are the only hands that will ever touch the steering wheel of your car. You are not in possession of any sort of driving manual and have no preconceived notions about anything.

Soon you are not alone. From your bone and your flesh, your Creator brings forth a helpmate (see Genesis 2:18; 21–25). Together, you find yourselves in an environment that is unfamiliar yet comfortable. Then you receive your first instructions from a source you can hear but not see.

It encourages you to "Be fruitful and multiply, and fill the earth, and subdue it; and rule over the fish of the sea and over the birds of the sky, and over every living thing that moves on the earth" (Genesis 1:28). It also tells you that you are free to move about and "From any tree of the garden you may eat freely; but from the tree of the knowledge of good and evil you shall not eat, for in the day that you eat from it you shall surely die" (Genesis 2:16–17).

In short order, you encounter a new, unknown influence, the serpent. It says, "The fruit of that forbidden tree won't kill you; on the contrary, it will make you wise like God, giving you the knowing of good and evil" (see Genesis 3:4–5). You wonder, *Is this good information*

31

or not? Is this source reliable? But wait a minute. What is good information? For that matter, what is bad information? And what makes this visible source of information more or less credible than our other source? More importantly, what is the meaning of good, and what is the meaning of evil? And death, what is death?

Lacking the "appropriate background knowledge" on any of these subjects, you make a decision based on prior experience. The garden you were in was full of trees with good-looking fruit that you had eaten before with no ill effect. This tree looked "good for food" and was a delight to the eyes, and, based upon your most recent source of information, its fruit was desirable to make one wise (see Genesis 3:6). So, having reasoned your way to a decision, you eat. You have committed the first acts of disobedience.

The Consequence

The apostle Paul tells us that it was as a result of this disobedience that "sin entered into the world and death through sin" (Romans 5:12a; see also 7:9–11). By the judgment of God (see Romans 5:16b), the human condition has now been altered. Staying with my narrative, you have suffered the spiritual death that had been forewarned. You are now no longer alone in your car. As a consequence of your disobedience, the spiritual presence and power of sin has now joined your God-breathed soul as a passenger in your car and will also have a presence in the cars of all who come after you.

It is a presence and power of will that has a purpose of its own. You are entirely unaware of this change in your human condition, although your reaction to the misstep validates it as a reality. Under the influence of your new passenger, your never-before-noticed nakedness now brings shame, and the previously-heard sound of your Creator walking in the garden now brings fear (see Genesis 3:8–10).

The road of life now bends outward from the garden and will be fraught with difficulty. For an extended period of time—until Moses—there will be no external road signs (laws) to direct you. Your primary GPS will be your God-protected faculties of reason, that is, conscience, and your newly acquired knowledge of good and evil, the law that has been newly written in your heart.

As we become fruitful and multiply, the collective conduct of humans so distresses our Creator that He is sorry, grieved that He made us (see Genesis 6:6), and very nearly brings an end to our existence. But through Noah, a single righteous man (see Genesis 6:9b), we survive our Creator's wrath, and the journey starts again.

In due time, our collective disobedience displeases our Creator yet again (see Genesis 11:1–9), and by His judgment, we are scattered into many languages and many cultures. Throughout the course of continuing human history, we will become many nations and continue to lose the battle of our individual and collective conscience to the passenger that is sin, which is consistently craftier and stronger than we are. But just as He did with Job (see Job 2:6), our God-breathed, God-protected inner self (see Genesis 2:7b) continues to motivate our faith to recognize, honor, and give thanks to a Higher Authority (see Romans 1:18–21).

A Special Nation

As the human journey continues, our Creator reveals more of Himself and begins to interact with one among us, Abraham, in special ways. Because of his "by faith" manner of living, Abraham and his seed are designated as the beginning of a great nation, a people the Creator will claim as "His own possession out of all the peoples who are on the face of the earth" (Deuteronomy 7:6b). We are among this nation.

From Abraham to Moses, our nation grows in number, yet the collective and repetitive disobedience, the falling short of the glory of God (see Romans 3:11, 23), continues. Despite our special relationship with the Creator, we strive and fall under the pervasive influence of the unrealized presence of sin riding with us in our car.

Then, through the Mosaic Law, our nation (which is Abraham's) receives and embraces directives from the Creator. Lacking understanding and despite our inability to fulfill the requirements of those new Laws consistently, with time, we mistakenly begin to measure our performance against them as the means by which we

THE GOSPEL YOU'VE NEVER HEARD

are individually attaining the righteousness the Creator desires.

Our disobedience continues, however, and despite His infliction of pain and suffering as a consequence, our Creator consistently urges us to return to Him. As an extension of mercy, He ordains a system of acceptable sacrifices that, from time to time, assuages the guilt of our conscience. However, by those very sacrifices year by year, we are reminded of our continuing sins (see Hebrews 10:3).

Among our nation, there are many like us whose faith is genuine and whose steadfast effort to live faithfully continues for generations despite this internal, difficult struggle. From Isaac and Jacob, through Joseph and Moses, Rahab, Gideon, Barak, Samson, Jephthah, David, and Samuel, and the prophets, our faithful living gains the Creator's approval. Yet, we do not have the power to break free from the contrary influence and control of our unwanted passenger.

In our despair, we begin to cry out for a clean heart and a renewed spirit (see Psalms 51:10). We are discovering the realities of the consequence of the original garden transgression and the judgment of condemnation (see Romans 5:16) that became the inheritance of all who came after that event. We are realizing that we are not alone in our car. Like Paul, we cry out, "Wretched man that I am! Who will set me free from the body of this death?" (Romans 7:24).

Finally, after some four thousand years of our life journey, the favorable year of our Creator arrives (see Isaiah 61:2; Luke 4:19). As a response to our cry (see Psalms 102:18–22), God sends His own Son as an offering for sin and, by that sacrifice, provides a means of redemption from His original judgment of condemnation.

Just as by the one transgression the power of sin had entered our car, so now, by one selfless act of righteousness, another passenger is ready to join us for the balance of our journey (see Romans 5:15–19). This passenger, however, is not like the first. He will only enter our car if we personally invite Him. We have but to believe and to ask (Romans 10:8–10). *or He chooses us*

The Story Continues: We Choose to Obey

We rejoice to hear our Creator's message of the redeeming sacrifice of His Son. Out of gratitude and a deep sense of need, we choose to become obedient. And in that moment, from our hearts, there comes a genuine faith confession. Now, a new passenger is invited and welcomed into our car. By the grace of God, the free gift of His Holy Spirit has entered our car and released us from the captivity (see Luke 4:18c) by which our first sin passenger was working his will in our lives. The first part of our journey has ended. We are no longer unregenerate.

Sin remains a passenger, but by the newly declared condemnation of God (see Romans 8:3c), it has defi-

THE GOSPEL YOU'VE NEVER HEARD

nitely been relegated to the back seat (see Matthew
16:23a). The Holy Spirit has entered our car, and in that
moment of entry, our spirit is made perfect forever (see
Hebrews 10:14). We are regenerated. The only carnality
that remains in us is entirely within our flesh, and we
are no longer spiritually attached to it in any way. Thus,
we can now be in spiritual oneness with the only power
in existence that is greater than the power of sin (see
1 John 4:4), the very power of the spirit of God. By the
law of the Spirit of life in Christ Jesus, which is a law of
freedom, we have been set free from the law of sin and
death (see Romans 8:2).

For four thousand years, we were all spiritually dead
in our trespasses and sins (see Ephesians 2:1), slaves
and subject to the power of sin in our car. Then, in one
miraculous moment of faith, we were saved from that
death by becoming one with Christ in the likeness of
His death and in the likeness of His resurrection (see
Romans 6:5). For "what the [Mosaic] Law could not do
[...] God *did*: sending His own Son in the likeness of sinful flesh and *as an offering* for sin, He condemned sin in
the flesh" (Romans 8:3). Our old human condition was
crucified with Him so that we would no longer be slaves
to sin, for he who has died is freed from sin (see Romans 6:6–7). "Therefore if any man is in Christ, *he is* a
new creature; the old things have passed away; behold,
new things have come" (2 Corinthians 5:17).

By faith, we have accepted God's grace gift, and, as
a result, our human condition has been changed. Our

car now has three spiritual passengers: our own God-breathed, God-protected soul as a constant driver, the newly arrived spirit of God ready to assist us, and the continuing presence of sin in the back seat. And for what purpose has God extended such a wonderful gift of forgiveness, freedom, and empowerment? Paul provides a clear answer for us in Romans 8:4–8:

> In order that the requirement of the Law might be fulfilled in us, who do not walk according to the flesh but according to the Spirit. For those who are according to the flesh set their minds on the things of the flesh, but those who are according to the Spirit the things of the Spirit. For the mind set on the flesh is death, but the mind set on the Spirit is life and peace, because the mind set on the flesh is hostile toward God; for it does not subject itself to the law of God, for it is not even able *to do so*; and those who are in the flesh cannot please God.

In paraphrase, and in keeping with our narrative, this is what Paul is making clear: the requirement of the law(s) of God, which is consistent obedience, is now entirely possible for those who are no longer subject to the once-dominant control of the sin passenger. The Holy Spirit has come to enable consistent obedience. Unfortunately, those who are still held captive by the sin passenger (those whose souls are still unregenerate) are simply unable to see consistent obedience as a necessity. But those who have been set free by accepting the Spirit should steadfastly choose to surrender control of the driving of their car to the guidance of that Spirit.

For the mind that continues to be set on the flesh and the things of the world is death, i.e., it continues to be a slave to sin. But the mind set on the things of the Spirit is life and peace and is able to enjoy the consistency of obedience through the driving power of that Spirit. The continuing mindset of unregenerate humanity is hostile toward God and to the idea of obedience to an authority higher than their own; they are unable to see things any differently. The reality is that in such a condition, they are unable, no matter what they do, to please God (see v. 8).

Remember, Paul's above verses denote the standard by which every human being who has ever lived will be judged. From God's perspective, the essential here and now priority and purpose of every human life is two-fold: 1) the initial priority is obedient living, and 2) as a matter of daily course, such living is to continue "until we all attain to the unity of the faith, and of the knowledge of the Son of God, to a mature man, to the measure of the stature which belongs to the fulness of Christ" (Ephesians 4:13).

From the very beginning of our road trip, the will of our Creator has been for us not just to recognize and desire to make the right turn over the wrong, but to experience a life of correct turns as the constant result of our choices (see 1 Peter 1:14–15). No matter how strong our desire in that regard, the four-thousand-year journey proved that the desire of our hearts could not consistently overcome the power of our indwelling sin passenger.

From the days of Moses, even though we genuinely embraced the righteous directives from our Creator, our failure to adhere to them consistently was not readily understood by us as a personal shortcoming. Rather, over time, they became a means of measuring comparative personal accomplishments. In his Ephesians letter, Paul explained the reality of the unregenerate human condition in this way:

> And you were dead in your trespasses and sins, in which you formally walked according to the course of this world, according to the prince of the power of the air, of the spirit that is now working in the sons of disobedience. Among them we too all formerly lived in the lusts of our flesh, indulging the desires of the flesh and of the mind, and were by nature children of wrath, even as the rest.
>
> **Ephesians 2:1–3**

Thankfully, our internal condition has changed because of the new passenger in our car. By the power of the indwelling Holy Spirit, we have been released from our law-induced bondage to sin and, as a result, are no longer "in the flesh but in...[s]pirit" (Romans 8:9a). And,

THE GOSPEL YOU'VE NEVER HEARD

"If Christ is in you, though the body is dead because of sin, yet the spirit is alive because of righteousness" (Romans 8:10). Our spirit, which had suffered by inheritance the forewarned death in the garden, is now alive and in possession of the very power by which God had raised Jesus from the dead. It is a Spirit of power that stands ready and willing and entirely capable of ensuring the future direction of our life's road trip (see Romans 8:11).

With the Lord in the car, we can now rightfully exclaim with the apostle Paul, "I can do all things through Him who strengthens me" (Philippians 4:13). It is now possible for our car to be driven in exactly the same way that His was driven. How? By surrendering control of the driving to Him (Galatians 2:20)!

Deliberations

Questions for Reflection or Group Study

1. What is the key to an accurate understanding of any communication? Why is the word "appropriate" so important to the objective of an accurate understanding?

2. What is your personal conviction regarding the presence of the power of sin within you? How would you describe it?

3. Consider your own allegorical car traveling through life. Who is in the car with you? What is the journey like? How often are you conscious of who is driving your car?

4. From God's gospel perspective, what is the two-fold priority and purpose of every human life? What has been your experience of God working the above priority in your life?

4

Thread of Truth

In their book *I Don't Have Enough Faith to Be an Atheist,* authors Norman L. Geisler and Frank Turek identified a list of questions. They referred to them as "the five most consequential questions in life"[1] and listed them as follows:

1. Origin: where did we come from?
2. Identity: who are we?
3. Meaning: why are we here?
4. Morality: how should we live?
5. Destiny: where are we going?[2]

To further their point, they also wrote that "what someone believes about God affects everything else that he or she believes,"[3] and thus, the yearning to know the answers to those questions.

It is not a new yearning. Thirteenth-century philosopher Thomas Aquinas expressed the same thing this way: "There is within every soul a thirst for happiness and meaning."[4] Best-selling contemporary author David Berlinski noted this: "A religious instinct is universal: It arises in every human being—hence the popular observation that there are no atheists in foxholes."[5] Were he alive today, I suspect the apostle Paul would affirm that this yearning evidences an inner awareness of God as a response to the wonders of His creation. It also affirms the DNA of the soul of every human being: we all emanate from a life-giving breath from the spirit of God (see Job 33:4).

Welsh theologian Matthew Henry once said that there were "none so deaf as those that will not hear. None so blind as those that will not see." The mere fact that the answers to life's most consequential questions are still being sought by many is reflective of a failure to accurately understand God's gospel communication. It is my sincerest hope that by the end of this book, you will know the answers to each of the above questions and that you will be able to declare, as did Job, "I have heard of Thee by the hearing of the ear; but now my eye sees Thee" (Job 42:5).

Living by Faith

One of the reasons the apostle Paul claimed an unashamed regard for the gospel (see Romans 1:16a) was that he understood it to be the revelation of the righteousness (justness) of God (see Romans 1:17a). He could see that from one person's faith to the next, the critical issue for God was always the living by faith: "as it is written, 'BUT THE RIGHTEOUS *man* SHALL LIVE BY FAITH'" (Romans 1:17b). Here Paul was quoting from the Old Testament book of Habakkuk. It is a book with which he had long been familiar. He cited it here with an entirely different understanding. It was an understanding he had received "through a revelation of Jesus Christ" (Galatians 1:12b).

Contrary to what he formerly thought, Paul's new understanding was that the righteous regard of God toward any living human being did not and would not come as a result of some measure of human performance against some divinely authored set of laws, e.g., the Ten Commandments (see Hebrews 7:19a). Rather, since the beginning of time, righteous recognition from God had been granted to those who had endeavored to live in accordance with what they could have and, therefore, should have known to be true as a result of the revelations of Him that were available to them during the time of their living. And, because of the work of the law written in the hearts of all human beings, the law of the knowledge of good and evil, at a minimum, all have experienced an interaction of conscience to some degree, "their thoughts alternately accusing or else defending them" (Romans 2:15b).

This is a foundational truth that is just as applicable to those who have embraced Christ as their Lord and Savior as it was to those whose faith in the justness of God was limited to the Old Testament witness of the Law and the prophets (see Romans 3:21–22) or, for an even greater portion of humanity, limited only to the evidence of His eternal power and divine nature visible from the beginning through the wonders of His creation (see Romans 1:19–20). Understanding what it means then to live by faith is a great place to begin the journey toward a proper understanding of the gospel message.

To Convince and Persuade

From time to time, throughout the balance of this book, I am going to provide definitions of certain words and/or phrases for purposes of better understanding what they mean when used within the context of the gospel. Throughout time, the original meanings these words were intended to convey have either been lost or, at a minimum, misunderstood.

The word "faith" in the phrase "live by faith" is the word *pistis* in Greek, which is from the root *peitho*, which means to "convince, persuade, [or] appeal to."[6] In its simplest form, particularly as it relates to God, *pistis* means believing that God is, that He does, in fact, exist. For example, Hebrews 11:6 says, "And without faith [*pistis*] it is impossible to please *Him*, for he who comes to God must believe that He is, and *that* He is a rewarder of those who seek Him."

From God's perspective, beneficial human conduct, conduct that is pleasing to Him, must begin with and be grounded in a belief that He exists. According to the

THE GOSPEL YOU'VE NEVER HEARD

apostle Paul, God's existence is the one thing that all human beings, from the beginning of time, have known:

> Because that which is known about God [at a minimum that He exists] is evident within them; for God made it evident to them. For since the creation of the world His invisible attributes, His eternal power and divine nature, have been clearly seen, being understood through what has been made, so that they are without excuse.
>
> **Romans 1:19–20**

Sam Harris has expressed considerable angst that there are "260 million Americans (87 percent of the population) who claim to 'never doubt the existence of God.'"[7] No human being (even Mr. Harris) is going to be able to stand in front of the Lord and declare as a credible defense, "But I never knew you existed." Instead, according to Paul's description in his next Romans verse, what will be made known in that judgment moment is that "even though they knew God, they did not honor Him as God, or give thanks; but they became futile in their speculations [e.g., there is no God], and their foolish heart was darkened" (v. 21).

More than Just Believing

However, the gospel is clear that the standard of God's justness requires far more than just believing that He exists. Within the phrase "live by faith," though

47

still *pistis* in Greek, that word "faith" takes on a meaning beyond just believing. In this instance, per Bauer's *Greek-English Lexicon*, it is used to represent "that which is believed, the body of faith or belief, doctrine; that which according to God's will is to be believed."[8] There is a basic *Webster's Dictionary* definition of faith that reads: "the assent of the mind to the truth of what is declared by another."[9] With slight modification and for purposes of better understanding the meaning of faith in this usage, the definition becomes: "the assent of the mind to the truth of what is (or has been) declared by God."

Now, in the light of that definition, consider again, "BUT THE RIGHTEOUS *man* SHALL LIVE BY FAITH" (Romans 1:17b). This verse does not say that the righteous man is the man who has faith, the man who simply believes that God exists. The Bible declares that even demons believe that there is one God, "and shudder" (James 2:19). Rather, what the verse is saying is that from God's perspective, the righteous man has been, is, and always will be the man who lives by faith. In other words, the righteous man is the man who holds himself accountable to a manner of living that reflects what he could have, and therefore, should have recognized over the course of his lifetime as true revelations of God.

The Bible identifies three successive time periods, each containing an expanded revelation of God and His truth. The first period began with God's Son existing before the creation of the world (see Colossians 1:15b;

THE GOSPEL YOU'VE NEVER HEARD

Revelation 3:14b) and continued through the Son with the creation of everything else, *"both* in the heavens and on earth, visible and invisible, whether thrones or dominions or rulers or authorities—all things have been created through Him and for Him" (Colossians 1:16).

During that first period of revelation, at a minimum, human beings were capable of acknowledging God's existence by honoring Him and giving thanks (see Romans 1:21). Virtually all historical records of human civilizations going as far back as they can be reliably determined affirm the worship of some kind of higher power or divine nature. Whether it was the sun, the moon, the stars, the mountains, a grandfather in the sky, ancestors, or some skillfully crafted rock, statue, or art form created from the mind of the worshipers, human beings have always worshiped a higher power.

To the extent that there are still such worshipers in the world today who have never been exposed to the gospel of our Lord, there is nothing disingenuous about their practices. Think of them as though they were among the seekers that the apostle Paul spoke to at the Areopagus or perhaps even as those who were being described by the prophet Micah when he wrote: "And what does the Lord require of you but to do justice, to love kindness, and to walk humbly with your God?" (Micah 6:8).

The second period encompassed God's interaction with Abraham, continued through the patriarchs and the deliverance of the Hebrews from Egypt guided by

49

Moses and culminated in the prophets. The apostle Paul refers to this period of God's special interaction with the nation of Israel as the righteousness of God that had been "witnessed by the Law and the Prophets" (Romans 3:21). Finally, there is the third time period and God's final revelation of truth, "the summing up of all things in Christ" (Ephesians 1:10b), or the fitting together of all three periods of revelation as one completed truth.

God's Consummate Communication

In each period of revelation, the consistency of God's justness is to be understood through the filter of the gospel of the Lord Jesus Christ. The rightness and hope of everything we believe and, thus, everything we do in this life is dependent upon a proper understanding of that gospel communication. Apart from that proper understanding, human nakedness, as first revealed in the Garden of Eden, still remains. You'll recall that Adam and Eve's first recognition of their nakedness, lack of covering, was right after they had eaten of the apple. Under the influence of the law that had just been written in their hearts, the law of the knowledge of good and evil, their immediate response was to cover themselves (see Genesis 3:7, 10–11).

This reference to their nakedness is metaphorically a reference to their lack of knowledge. It was their lack of knowledge that actually led to their fall in the first place (more on that in the chapter "The Big Picture"). It

THE GOSPEL YOU'VE NEVER HEARD

is that remaining human nakedness or lack of knowledge that mankind has been trying to cover since that first moment in the garden. Unfortunately, as was noted by Isaiah, apart from the knowledge of Christ, the best that anyone can do is to cover him or herself with a filthy garment (see Isaiah 64:6), a garment made according to the thought of man.

In an earlier chapter, there was a reference to a thread of unbroken truth that runs through the Bible, all the way from the first word in Genesis to the last word in Revelation. Here we see that it is in the light of the proper understanding of the gospel that truth is revealed. The psalmist wrote, "Give me understanding according to Thy word" (Psalms 119:169). The Lord Jesus said, "If you abide in My word, *then* you are truly disciples of Mine; and you shall know the truth, and the truth shall make you free" (John 8:31b–32).

The truth has been revealed. And it was affirmed as reliable the moment Jesus rose from the dead. Read what He tells us:

> The Amen, the faithful and true Witness, the Beginning of the creation of God, says this [...] Because you say, "I am rich, and have become wealthy, and have need of nothing," and you do not know that you are wretched and miserable and poor and blind and naked, I advise you to buy from Me gold refined by fire, that you may become rich, and white garments, that you may

clothe yourself, and *that* the shame of your nakedness may not be revealed; and eyesalve to anoint your eyes, that you may see.

Revelation 3:14b, 17–18

He is telling us to put Him on as a garment (see also Romans 13:14). He is the only cloth that can cover our nakedness, and we can know for certain that such nakedness, lack of understanding, is not a virtue. Nevertheless, in this life, each of us is free to thread our needles and stitch our garments with whatever we choose to identify as truth. However, what must be equally understood is that the choices we make, particularly regarding truth, have significant consequences. A "white garment" can and, according to Jesus, must be stitched. Let's grab hold of the unbroken thread of real truth and start sewing.

THE GOSPEL YOU'VE NEVER HEARD

Deliberations
Questions for Reflection or Group Study

1. What should a true child of God know about the answers to life's most consequential questions (see John 1:9; 8:12)? Should those questions still be considered unanswerable? Why or why not?
2. Define faith. Is there a difference between "having faith" and "living by faith"? What is it?
3. From the beginning, at a minimum, what is it that God has required of all human beings (see Romans 1:21)? What is it about the history of human cultures that affirms this activity? What do you hear when you read Micah 6:8?
4. Reread Revelation 3:14b, 17–18. Try to read these verses as though the Lord were speaking them directly to you in this very moment. What is He calling His audience (the lukewarm members of the church in Laodicea) to recognize? What is He advising them to do to resolve their malady? Is this instruction applicable in today's world?

5

Beyond Confusion

In his first letter to the church at Corinth, the apostle Paul made it very clear that there was only one foundation upon which a person should be living his or her life: "for no man can lay a foundation other than the one which is laid, which is Jesus Christ" (1 Corinthians 3:11). Any good home builder will tell you that a firm foundation requires solid footings. Think of the next several chapters as the examination of those footings, the ones upon which the one and true foundation rests. Myths are made of sand. These footings are not made of sand. By digging deeply into the core knowledge of these biblical footings, we will realize that the information necessary to the understanding of truth has indeed been revealed.

As I noted in the chapter "The Concealed Now Revealed," I agree with the point Sam Harris made regarding individual beliefs. Good arguments are the basis for adopted beliefs. There is no better authority for the making of a good and trustworthy truth argument

THE GOSPEL YOU'VE NEVER HEARD

than the Word of God, precisely because it is the Word of God.

In the pages that follow, there will be a steady diet of biblical references. I encourage you to slow down when you read them. They are critically essential to the objective of explaining "the way of God more accurately" (Acts 18:26). May each of us embrace these truths with a sincere curiosity, find them easy to digest, and discover that they are sweeter than honey to our taste (see Psalms 119:103). Remember, from God's perspective, man was not created to live on bread alone. The fact that we can does not diminish the reality and importance of that truth.

Can We Really Know?

There is a common perception that comprehending the thoughts of God goes beyond the limits of the human mind. Invariably citing the following verses from Isaiah, chapter fifty-five, theologians and Bible teachers have created a "but we can't really know" or "we can't really be sure" mindset:

> For My thoughts are not your thoughts, neither are your ways My ways," declares the LORD. "For *as* the heavens are higher than the earth, so are My ways higher than your ways, and My thoughts than your thoughts.
>
> **Isaiah 55: 8–9**

Such an interpretation from these two verses is a misunderstanding of Isaiah's message. It needs to be corrected. Read them again, this time within the context of the preceding and following verses:

> Seek the LORD while He may be found; call upon Him while He is near. Let the wicked forsake his way, and the unrighteous man his thoughts; and let him return to the LORD, and He will have compassion on him; and to our God, for He will abundantly pardon. "For My thoughts are not your thoughts, neither are your ways My ways," declares the LORD. "For *as* the heavens are higher than the earth, so are My ways higher than your ways, and My thoughts than your thoughts." For as the rain and the snow come down from heaven, and do not return there without watering the earth, and making it bear and sprout, and furnishing seed to the sower and bread to the eater; so shall My word be which goes forth from My mouth; it shall not return to Me empty, without accomplishing what I desire, and without succeeding *in the matter* for which I sent it.
>
> **Isaiah 55: 6–11**

Nowhere in these verses is Isaiah saying that a person's inability to comprehend the thoughts and ways of God is a permanent condition. Rather, Isaiah's admonition in the passage is to the unrighteous man whose

THE GOSPEL YOU'VE NEVER HEARD

spiritual condition of captivity to the indwelling presence of sin prevented him from understanding the ways of God.

As I noted in the previous chapter, this was the pre-Christ condition of all human beings that was referenced by Paul early in his Romans letter when he quoted from the psalmist, "THERE IS NONE RIGHTEOUS, NOT EVEN ONE; THERE IS NONE WHO UNDERSTANDS" (Romans 3:10–11a). The "good news" of the gospel is that faith in Christ Jesus changes a believer's spiritual condition and thereby eliminates what had previously been the unrighteous man's impediment to understanding.

We Are Either Regenerate or Unregenerate

As referenced in my earlier allegorical narrative, it is important to recognize that from God's perspective and by His design, there are only two spiritual conditions in which human beings can exist: "regenerate" and "unregenerate." Let me explain the origin of the terms. Early in the sixteenth century, the word "regenerate" was used regarding someone who had been spiritually reborn by a confession of faith in Christ and had thereby received the indwelling presence of the Holy Spirit. Typically, when used today, the word "regenerate" references the spiritual condition of someone who is said to have been "born again" (see John 3:3).

By the end of that same century, "English speakers had added 'un' to 'regenerate' to describe someone who refused to accept spiritual reformation."[1] "Unregenerate" or "natural" references the condition of spiritual bondage into which all human beings were born post the fall of Adam.

As the Scripture says: "through one transgression there resulted [God-determined] condemnation to all men" (Romans 5:18a). From a spiritual perspective, it is referred to as an inherited death (see Romans 5:12–14), and it is precisely the death that God warned of should Adam and Eve eat of the forbidden fruit (see Genesis 2:16–17). There is no escape from this spiritual death except by a confession of faith in the Lord Jesus Christ (see Acts 4:12).

The inherent limitations of understanding that fell to the unregenerate no longer apply to the regenerate. The apostle Paul himself wrote of these limitations: "But a natural [unregenerate] man does not accept the things of the Spirit of God; for they are foolishness to him, and he cannot understand them, because they are spiritually appraised" (1 Corinthians 2:14). But the gospel of the Lord Jesus Christ has made clear that what was unknowable for a natural man has become entirely knowable for the born-again, regenerate man.

Perpetuating the concept that the thoughts of God are not knowable to those who truly love Him denies the truth of what the knowledge contained in the gospel declares. The Word of God, again through Paul, explains it best:

THE GOSPEL YOU'VE NEVER HEARD

And my message and my preaching were not in persuasive words of wisdom, but in demonstration of the Spirit and of power, that your faith should not rest on the wisdom of men, but on the power of God. Yet, we do speak wisdom among those who are mature; a wisdom, however, not of this age [age of unregenerate men], nor of the rulers of this age, who are passing away; but we speak God's wisdom in a mystery, the hidden *wisdom*, which God predestined before the ages to our glory; *the wisdom* which none of the rulers of this age has understood; for if they had understood it, they would not have crucified the Lord of glory; but just as it is written:

"THINGS WHICH EYE HAS NOT SEEN AND EAR HAS NOT HEARD, AND *which* HAVE NOT ENTERED THE HEART OF MAN, ALL THAT GOD HAS PREPARED FOR THOSE WHO LOVE HIM."

For to us God revealed *them* through the Spirit; for the Spirit searches all things, even the depths of God. For who among men knows the *thoughts* of a man except the spirit of the man, which is in him? Even so the *thoughts* of God no one knows except the Spirit of God. Now we have received, not the spirit of the world, but the Spirit who is from God, that we might know the things freely given to us by God, which things we also speak, not in words taught by human wisdom, but in those taught by the Spirit, combining spiritual *thoughts* with spir-

itual *words* [...] For WHO HAS KNOWN THE MIND OF
THE LORD, THAT HE SHOULD INSTRUCT HIM? But
we have the mind of Christ.

1 Corinthians 2:4–13, 16

In and through the power of the indwelling Holy
Spirit, the regenerate person can not only know
thoughts from the very depths of God, he or she can
also understand them.

My own faith-life journey has taught me that such
an understanding is not gained by osmosis or by mere
possession of the Holy Spirit. In fact, "all the wealth that
comes from the full assurance of understanding, *resulting* in a true knowledge of God's mystery, *that is*, Christ
Himself, in whom are hidden all the treasures of wisdom and knowledge" (Colossians 2:2b–3) is not made
clear to a person at the moment of conversion. It is only
to be gained during a lifetime of presenting oneself to
the Lord and His word, as "a living and holy sacrifice
[...] [to] be transformed by the renewing of your mind,
that you may prove what the will of God is, that which
is good and acceptable and perfect" (Romans 12:1–2).
From a personal standpoint, doing so with patience,
steadfastness, and a sincere hunger has been my most
appropriate application of Mr. Cheever's life lesson.

Knowing and Understanding Is Possible

According to the Bible, knowing and understanding
the mind of Christ is possible. In James, chapter one,
verses five through eight, we read:

THE GOSPEL YOU'VE NEVER HEARD

> But if any of you lacks wisdom, let him ask of God, who gives to all men generously and without reproach, and it will be given to him. But let him ask in faith without any doubting, for the one who doubts is like the surf of the sea driven and tossed by the wind. For let not that man expect that he will receive anything from the Lord, *being* a double-minded man, unstable in all his ways.

Even Jesus reflected a similar word of instruction: "My teaching is not Mine, but His who sent Me. If any man is willing to do His will, he shall know of the teaching" (John 7:16b–18).

Our misguided teaching regarding the unknowability of the thoughts of God has contributed to why the Bible has been and is still so little read and even less studied. The key to knowing and experiencing the true teachings of the Lord must include regular and consistent meetings with Him in the Bible (see John 8:31b–32). It should be done directly, and it should be done with a full conviction of the heart (see Jeremiah 29:13). Most importantly, we should regard it as something that is mandatory, not optional.

Perhaps what is most difficult for us is that the approach should be as that of a trusting child (see Luke 18:17). When we meet with the Lord in His word, we should come to Him not as self-confident intellects but rather as innocent children thirsting for learning. To approach Him in any other way is to be double-minded. Seeking to know His thoughts while refusing to surrender our own will prove to be unproductive (see James 1:6–8).

If we are faithful and persevere with patience, then the result will be just as the apostle John predicted:

> And as for you, the anointing which you received from Him abides in you, and you have no need for anyone to teach you; but as His anointing teaches you about all things and is true and is not a lie, and just as it has taught you, you abide in Him. And now little children, abide in Him, so that when He appears, we may have confidence and not shrink away from Him in shame at his coming.
>
> **1 John 2:27–28**

I was sixteen years into my faith-life journey before I realized that my relationship with the Bible was, at best, casual. It wasn't because I didn't know what it meant to be totally committed to something. As a life-long athlete, I had spent a good deal of my time immersed in playbooks and game plans while enduring endless hours of practice. I did this because I knew there was no shortcut to being the best athlete I could be in any given game situation. We all have things in this life for which we go the extra mile. The Bible should be paramount among those things.

THE GOSPEL YOU'VE NEVER HEARD

Ultimately, the truth of biblical teaching lies in the words that were written, not in the charisma of the voice from the pulpit, the leader of your Bible study, or the words in the pages of this book. The Bible's words are not just ordinary words. They are words of wisdom and power (see 1 Corinthians 1:24; 2:4–5). We must endeavor to hide those words in our hearts if we hope to be living as God intends (see Psalms 119:11), and we must be examining ourselves daily to make sure that our manner of living is a constant reflection of those words. For as long as we breathe, we must seek to live continuously as the student, not the Teacher, as the reader, not the Author, as the player, not the Coach.

For many, in-depth Bible study may be unfamiliar territory. It certainly was for me. But by embracing that approach, I was able to discover the appropriate background knowledge that made the Bible come alive for me. "Filing Paperwork" became "Washing Clothes," and it made my relationship with the Lord become something altogether different than it had ever been.

In Romans, chapter eight, Paul wrote, "The Spirit Himself bears witness with our spirit that we are children of God" (v. 16). I have never heard an audible word from the Lord, but I have conversations with Him all the time. His voice is in my thoughts, and, more times than not, I know them to be His thoughts. It wasn't always that way for me, but as I committed to hiding His word in my heart, He began to speak to me with those very words. As I look forward to the day when I will be standing before Him, I am comforted knowing that we will not be meeting each other for the first time.

I often wondered how Paul could write of "taking every thought captive to the obedience of Christ" (2 Corinthians 10:5). I now know what he meant. Indeed, my relationship with my Bible is no longer casual. It has become my dearest possession and my most important nourishment. Confusion, doubt, and disappointment no longer reign in my faith life. "It is written, 'MAN SHALL NOT LIVE ON BREAD ALONE, BUT ON EVERY WORD THAT PROCEEDS OUT OF THE MOUTH OF GOD'" (Matthew 4:4).

I have found this to be completely true.

THE GOSPEL YOU'VE NEVER HEARD

Deliberations

Questions for Reflection or Group Study

1. Do you find the idea of being able to know and understand the thoughts of God comforting or disquieting? Why? According to the apostle Paul, how is it that we can know the "thoughts of God," the very thoughts that originate from the "mind of Christ" (see 1 Corinthians 2:4–13, 16)?

2. What are the two terms used to describe the only two spiritual conditions in which human beings exist? Explain the difference between them.

3. What should our attitude be as we present ourselves to the spiritual words that represent the spiritual thoughts that emanate from the mind of Christ? How does this activity capture the idea of being transformed by "the renewing of your mind" (see Romans 12:1–2)?

4. Identify the things in your life for which you have unquestionably gone the "extra mile." Consider what motivated you to expend the extra effort. Does the amount of time you currently spend in the Bible validate it as a priority in your life? Share or journal what changes, if any, you might need to make.

6

Universal Inheritance

I am convinced that the true knowledge of God's mystery—that is, the true knowledge of Christ Himself—has been replaced generally with a doctrine designed to tickle the ear; it is a doctrine that has prevented people from knowing the truth as God intended it to be known and understood. Therefore, I am certain that what I am writing will challenge the current core beliefs of many. Such a challenge is meant to bring clarity in the midst of confusion, and considering what is at stake, it may be a good thing for those beliefs to be challenged (see 2 Timothy 2:15).

This is not a matter of one opinion as opposed to another opinion. It is not a matter of my opinion as opposed to another. We need to know God's opinion. There is only one place to find His opinion. The truth of the Bible, contrary to the pride of the human intellect, has never been a matter of the varying opinions of that intellect.

The truth has always been a predetermined fact established by the mind of God. And His mind is not divided. To learn that while in this life is better than when standing in front of the only begotten Son of the Author. If we have not contemplated the reality of that as a future event, we need to do so. It will ultimately come for all of us.

An Early Lesson from Job

There is a lesson from the book of Job that proved very helpful in directing me toward the discovery of the one opinion I was seeking. The book is the story of a man who suffered great tragedy "without cause" (see Job 2:2c). It is important to note that he lived during a time that was without a written Word of God. The prevailing faith perspective of his day had been formed as a response to the experience of life itself.

It was a perspective that theologians refer to as "retribution theology." In short, "retribution theology holds that people are treated by God based on how they behave."[1] If you suffer, it is because there is unconfessed sin in your life; if you prosper, it is because you are living in a manner that is pleasing to God. As we will see, it was a wrong perspective.

Nevertheless, it was the prevailing understanding of Job's day. When Job's tragedies befell him, three of his closest friends and even his wife call him out (more on this in the next chapter). First, from his wife, he is told that he should stop holding to his feigned integrity, and instead, "Curse God and die!" (2:9). Indeed, quite a rebuke from a wife!

Then, the first of his friends, Eliphaz, comes forward and validates the thinking of the day with these words:

> Remember now, who *ever* perished being innocent? Or where were the upright destroyed? According to what I have seen, those who plow iniquity and those who sow trouble harvest it. By the breath of God they perish, and by the blast of His anger they come to an end.
>
> **Job 4:7–9**

Bildad is the next friend to speak, and in a similar manner, he begins with this:

> Does God pervert justice or does the Almighty pervert what is right? If your sons sinned against Him, then He delivered them into the power of their transgression. If you would seek God and implore the compassion of the Almighty, if you are pure and upright, surely now He would rouse Himself for you and restore your righteous estate.
>
> **Job 8:3–6**

Can you imagine having a best friend tell you that the reason you lost all ten of your children is because they were all sinners?

THE GOSPEL YOU'VE NEVER HEARD

But it is what Bildad said next that introduced me to what would affirm my method of study:

> Please inquire of past generations, and consider the things searched out by their fathers. For we are *only* of yesterday and know nothing, because our days on earth are as a shadow, will they not teach you *and* tell you, and bring forth words from their minds?
>
> **Job 8:8–10**

Bring forth words from *their* minds...bring forth words from *their* minds. How good was that advice? I will let God's words speak from the last chapter of the Job story:

> And it came about after the LORD had spoken these words to Job, that the LORD said to Eliphaz the Temanite, "My wrath is kindled against you and against your two friends [Bildad and Zophar], because you have not spoken of Me what is right as My servant Job has. Now therefore, take for yourselves seven bulls and seven rams, and go to My servant Job, and offer up a burnt offering for yourselves, and My servant Job will pray for you. For I will accept him so that I may not do with you *according to your* folly, because you have not spoken of Me what is right, as My servant Job has.
>
> **Job 42:7–8**

As regards the true meaning of the gospel of the Lord Jesus Christ, it became clear to me that the discord that has been evident throughout the centuries, and remains even yet today, is largely a result of far too much reliance on the thinking "of past generations." Jesus did not say that we could know the meaning and purpose of His life by relying on the teaching of others, however helpful it might be. He said we could know it by relying on Him! "For the Scripture says, 'WHOEVER BELIEVES IN HIM WILL NOT BE DISAPPOINTED'" (Romans 10:11).

The Importance of Word Meanings

In order to understand the New Testament as God intended, I have found that study and analysis of word meanings in original Greek can help to ensure that the intentional message, within His unbroken thread of truth, is not lost in translation. For example, on numerous occasions, the apostle Paul prayed for those to whom he was writing. Two such occasions reflect a consistent theme in his prayers regarding the word "knowledge."

In Colossians, chapter one, he wrote,

> we have not ceased to pray for you and to ask that you may be filled with the knowledge of His will in all spiritual wisdom and understanding, so that you may walk in a manner worthy of the Lord, to please *Him* in all respects, bearing fruit in

THE GOSPEL YOU'VE NEVER HEARD

every good work and increasing in the knowledge of God.

vv. 9–10

Similarly, in his letter to Philemon, he wrote,

and I pray that the fellowship of your faith [the internal thought interaction between a believer and the Holy Spirit] may become effective through the knowledge of every good thing which is in you for Christ's sake.

Philemon 1:6

Even the apostle Peter referenced the same knowledge in this way: "seeing that His divine power has granted to us everything pertaining to life and godliness, through the true knowledge of Him who called us by His own glory and excellence" (2 Peter 1:3).

Understanding the Meaning of Knowledge

The word "knowledge" in these verses is translated from the Greek word *epignosis*, which is from the root *gnosis* ("knowledge"; "that which is knowable"). *Epignosis* denotes "a larger and more thorough knowledge; it is a full and exact knowledge."[2] These verses make clear that possessing a fuller, more exact knowledge of "God's mystery, *that is,* Christ *Himself*" (Colossians 2:2b) is the key to being able to "walk in a manner worthy of the Lord, to please *Him* in all respects" (Colossians

71

1:10a). We live in the time of the gospel of Christ. Our best chance of hearing, "Well done good and faithful slave [servant]" (see Matthew 25:23a) is to endeavor to live our lives in accordance with the full and exact knowledge that was revealed in that gospel.

In his book *Beyond Seduction*, Dave Hunt wrote, "This desire seems to be largely lacking in the contemporary church. As a consequence, there is a defective knowledge of God."[3] I was two decades into my faith-life journey before I realized the knowledge I'd originally received stood on defective footings. We must make every effort to be certain that what we believe to be true regarding the gospel is supported by footings that are not built on sand.

Historical theological scholarship has consistently affirmed that Paul's letter to the Romans is "the fullest and most coherent manifesto of the Christian Gospel in the New Testament."[4] It has also been referred to as:

> The chief book of the New Testament and the purest Gospel [...] the profoundest book in existence [...] the greatest and richest of all the apostolic works [...] the cathedral of the Christian faith [...] the most remarkable production of the most remarkable man.[5]

By itself, it doesn't represent "the whole message of this Life" (Acts 5:20b), but it most certainly lays the foundation of understanding upon which the whole of the gospel message must rest, a foundation that must be carefully established. As you will see, it was in the heart of this letter that I spent a good deal of time listening.

How the Apostle Paul Gained Understanding

Before looking at selected parts of this Romans letter, it is important to note how Paul gained the understanding of what he refers to in the letter as "my gospel" (Romans 2:16a; 16:25a). By the time he wrote this letter, he had been preaching for some twenty years. His faith, or understanding, was not of his own making. It was not a product of his considerable human intellect. "For I would have you know, brethren," he wrote, "that the gospel which was preached by me is not according to man. For I neither *received it* from man, nor was I taught it, but I received it through a revelation of Jesus Christ" (Galatians 1:11–12).

For Paul, the gospel that he preached was not a matter of his opinion or that of anyone else's. From his earliest childhood, he had been "brought up [...] in the straitest sect of the [Jewish] religion [...] Everything [he had learned] tended to prepare him to be an eminent member of that theological party."[6] By his own admission, he had been "advancing in Judaism beyond many of my contemporaries among my countrymen, being more extremely zealous for my ancestral traditions" (Galatians 1:14).

73

He had undoubtedly come to see himself as a defender of those traditions, and as such, he had become a persecutor of the church (see Philippians 3:6a). But by divine revelation, he was completely transformed in his thinking. His Romans letter is more than just a personal recounting of a casual occurrence. It is a detailing of a lesson from the heart of a student who had been directly taught by the only One any of us are to call "Teacher" (see Matthew 23:8; John 13:13–14). It is a very reliable written testimony of the framework truth of the gospel. It is of benefit to study and trust it.

It is no small thing to note the bookends of Paul's letter. He begins and ends with the reason for his preaching of the gospel: "to bring about *the* obedience of faith" (Romans 1:5b) and *"leading* to the obedience of faith" (Romans 16:26c). There is nothing the Bible reveals and affirms more consistently from beginning to end than 1) God's desire for obedience from His children (see 1 Samuel 15:22–23) and 2) His revealed (see Romans 1:18) and/or as-yet-to-be revealed (see Romans 2:5) wrath as a consequence of disobedience.

It is a tone that was set in the story of the entrance of sin into the human experience (see Genesis 3), and it is a tone that remained constant throughout biblical history. From Adam to Moses and the prophets and from Moses and the prophets to Christ, God's desire for obedience and mankind's inability to comply consistently were a universal constant, the reality of which Paul addresses from Romans 1:18 through 3:20.[7]

The Cause of Our Disobedience

The history of the specifics of that repetitive disobedience is not the focus of Paul's continued writing in Romans. He turns his writing to the more specific aspects of the gospel that are critical to an accurate understanding. In Romans 7, he explains the cause of that disobedience and how it was identified, and in Romans 8, he reveals the glorious good news regarding the remedy: how obedient living can now be consistently accomplished.

It is important to remember that though this letter was written nearly two thousand years ago to the believers in Rome, it could just as well have been written to us yesterday because God's desired objective of obedient living has not changed. From His perspective, the consistency of obedience in this life is the prerequisite toward maturity, "until we all attain to the unity of the faith [...] to the measure of the stature which belongs to the fulness of Christ" (see Ephesians 4:13).

Why such an emphasis on obedient living? Because His broader and certain will for all of mankind is to be living in a manner that is a constant reflection of His glory (see 2 Corinthians 3:18) and His holiness (see 1 Peter 1:14–17).

Romans, chapter seven, brings to light the inherited unregenerate condition of every human being since Adam, irrespective of the culture or religion, or century into which that person was born. Any advancement of mankind during the subsequent centuries, intellectual or otherwise, has not changed anything in that regard. A reasonably good descriptive definition of this universally inherited human condition was put forth by the World Transformation Movement. It reads,

> The human condition is the subconscious sense of guilt and agony we each carry of being unable to explain humans' contradictory capacity for immense love and sensitivity on one hand, and greed, hatred, brutality, rape, murder and war on the other. While the universally accepted ideals are to be *cooperative, loving and selfless*, humans are variously *competitive, aggressive and selfish*—and our inability to understand this paradox has been the burden of human life; it has been our human condition.[8]

The Glorious Remedy

Romans, chapter eight, describes the glorious remedy to this condition. It is the only remedy (see Acts 4:12) that God has made available for an inherited human condition that causes all to "fall short of the glory of God" (Romans 3:23b). One day the whole of humanity will be standing in front of the One whose personal sacrifice was the remedy for mankind's unregenerate human condition. It is a wise investment of time to be diligently seeking to understand the significance of Christ's sacrifice and the effect He hoped it would have on all who would believe in His name (see John 8:11).

THE GOSPEL YOU'VE NEVER HEARD

I want to digress for a moment to interject something from Jesus. On a number of occasions, Jesus would follow something He had just said with the statement: "He who has ears to hear, let him hear" (Matthew 11:15; 13:9, 43; also Mark 4:23; Luke 8:8; 14:35). It was His way of emphasizing not only the importance of what He had just explained but also the need for His listeners to comprehend that importance. In other words, if they weren't paying attention, they should have been!

Over the course of my athletic career, on many occasions, I heard, "Guys, pay attention!" It was the signal that the next instruction was critical to success. I don't mean to suggest that anyone's reading attentiveness has been less than adequate to this point. It's just that the next four chapters of my writing will be intensely focused on some critically important parts of Paul's letter. It is what the Lord taught me from these chapters that led to the reformation of my gospel understanding. It made me realize that what I had previously been led to believe was not accurate. It was a discovery that was aided by my heightened desire to hear. As I begin to delve into these critical chapters, I would be remiss if I neglected to signal, "Reader, pay attention!"

Law: Its Use and Meaning

By the time of this writing of Romans, there can be no doubt that Paul's preaching experience made him aware of those points that had been hard for his listeners to comprehend. Among those difficult points was understanding the purpose of a new covenant. Especially for those who had come out of the Jewish faith tradition, understanding the purpose of a new agreement between God and man was a challenging task.

As we begin to consider Paul's answers as to the purpose of both the old and the new covenants, it is important that we remember the following: as regards both covenants, "it was God alone who set the conditions."[9] Paul's lesson plan is not of his own making, it is from the mind of God.

Paul's teachings regarding the place of the Law (see Exodus 20:1–17) in the light of the new covenant shook the very foundation of the Jewish faith. Their possession of the Law had been vital to their identity as the chosen of God. Having Paul tell them that their right of circumcision and their possession of the Law was not what made them Jewish was a very difficult pill for them to swallow (see Romans 2:25–29). He realized it was an issue that needed further explanation, and he had been perfectly educated for the task.

We will be better prepared to understand his teaching, particularly in chapter seven of the letter, if we make a brief but important note regarding his use of the word "law." In Greek, it is the word *nomos*. It appears seventy-six times (NASB translation) throughout the Romans letter, which is more than twice that of any other New Testament writing.

It is important to recognize that with his consistent use of the same word (exception: 2:12, *anomōs*, used

THE GOSPEL YOU'VE NEVER HEARD

twice), Paul was not implying the same meaning in every instance. In Romans, chapter seven alone, it appears twenty-two times (NASB) and not always with the same meaning. The meaning of Paul's use of the word is determined by the context. As we begin examining the verses, I will draw attention to that context and his meaning in each usage.

As a final and somewhat more generalized thought, whenever we encounter the word "law" within the context of Scripture, we are well-served if we start from the perspective that our ability to recognize any line between right and wrong is born from the law that was initially written in the hearts of all humanity, the law of the knowledge of good and evil (Romans 2:14–15).

Over the course of human history, God has utilized mankind's awareness of that defining line ("law") to enhance our understanding of the difference between right and wrong in one of the following three ways: (1) most famously, by the writing of His own hand directly, the Ten Commandments, (2) through His engagement with the mind of Moses and the other writers of Scripture, or (3) via the God-established, God-protected conscience of human beings as they endeavored to further define, or draw lines (laws), between the good and evil of their living experience.

In his marvelous three-volume work *Historical and Theological Foundations of Law*, John Eidsmoe notes this about the foundational law:

79

God gave the Ten Commandments to Moses, carved in stone, around 1450 B.C. as recorded in Exodus 20. But the rudiments of the Ten Commandments appear much earlier than that, as natural law written upon the hearts of man (Romans 2:14–15).[10]

And in support of this thought, Eidsmoe cites Martin Luther as follows:

The Decalogue is not of Moses, nor did God give it to him first. On the contrary, the Decalogue belongs to the whole world; it was written and engraved in the minds of all human beings from the beginning of the world.[11]

Even what we know of the antediluvian (pre-flood) period reflects the influence of this foundational law on the thinking of mankind. And not with a positive result. Noting that "the wickedness of man was great on the earth, and that every intent of the thoughts of his heart was only evil continually" (Genesis 6:5), Moses records an astonishing reflection of God when he writes, "And the Lord was sorry that He had made man on the earth, and He was grieved in His heart" (Genesis 6:6).

God's sorrow affirms that there must have been another choice for mankind to be making, and (thankfully) it is a choice that was realized in Noah. We will see that this foundational law plays a significant role

THE GOSPEL YOU'VE NEVER HEARD

in the writings of Paul. I will draw attention to it when appropriate.

Out with the Old, In with the New

The old covenant had established the Law (Torah[12]) as the cornerstone of the Jewish faith, the very glory upon which it had stood since the days of Moses. Not knowing about God's true righteousness (see Romans 10:3a), Israel saw the Law, and its own performance against it, as its means of attaining the righteousness of God. But now, in this new teaching, it was made clear that the true righteousness of God was not attainable through the Law based on human achievement.

Rather, the new covenant shows that the true righteousness of God is "that which is through faith in Christ, the righteousness which *comes* from God on the basis of faith" (Philippians 3:9b). What had originally been revealed with glory "in letters engraved on stones" (2 Corinthians 3:7a) had now been diminished and replaced by what the gospel revealed as an even greater glory (see 2 Corinthians 3:7–11). The old covenant had proven insufficient toward the objective of obedience and was therefore replaced by a new covenant, which offered the possibility of full and complete obedience.

In an effort to bring about a proper understanding of the relationship between the old and the new, Paul wrote of the ministries or purposes of both. In Romans, chapter seven, he writes of the old, the ministry of the Law that reveals the contradictory capacity of the human condition that had been the burden of human life. In chapter eight, he writes of the new, the ministry of the Spirit that reveals how the condition can be overcome and, as a result, how obedient living can be realized more effectively from one day to the next (see Matthew 6:33–34).

Before Paul begins with his description of the ministry of the Law, he reminds his readers in Romans, chapter six, that as a result of their faith in Christ, they have died to sin and have been released from their captivity to it (see Romans 6:7; also Luke 4:17–21). In the light of this new freedom, they are to "present [themselves] to God as those alive from the dead and [their bodies] *as* instruments of righteousness to God" (Romans 6:13b).

Questions for Each of Us

Are we familiar with what it means to have died to or to have been released from captivity to the indwelling presence of sin? Do we realize that such a death or release from captivity is a necessity for any person whose greatest desire is to be living life consistently in accordance with the revealed will of God?

It is extremely sad that after nearly two thousand years of gospel preaching, very few of the Americans who claim to "never doubt the existence of God"[13] understand that absent a genuine confession of faith in the Lord Jesus Christ, every living human being (from a spiritual perspective) is actually "dead in [his or her] trespasses and sins" (Ephesians 2:1).

THE GOSPEL YOU'VE NEVER HEARD

Despite the freedoms of choice and thought and expression that the living of life readily affirms, the reality is that apart from Christ, every living human being is spiritually dead and being held captive by the sin presence within them. It is important to emphasize that this spiritually dead condition is not a reference to what is going to happen to someone on the day he or she stands before the Lord. Even those who have genuinely embraced Christ as Lord, and thereby have been spiritually released from the internal death grip of sin (see Luke 4:18b), still have the presence of sin within them and will have until their earthly death.

This is why the battle between the flesh and the Spirit remains a reality even in the life of a born-again believer. But the new certainty with Christ in our lives is this: it is no longer a battle that we have to fight! We have only to learn how to let the Lord fight (and win) the daily battle for us (see Galatians 5:16–25).

The Bible makes clear that all human beings, despite the presence of indwelling sin, are possessors of the inherited knowledge of good and evil (see Genesis 3:22). It is evidenced by "the work of the Law written in [our] hearts, [our] conscience bearing witness, and [our] thoughts alternately accusing or else defending [our actions]" (Romans 2:15). Thus, we can discern the difference between right and wrong and freely desire the good over the evil. But apart from Christ (see John 15:15c) and a clear understanding of God's desired objective of holiness (see Leviticus 11:44–47; 19:2; 20:7),

83

what no one has—not even one—is the ability to consistently overcome the power and contrary influence of the sin that is within us.

As previously noted, what God desires from all of humanity is nothing short of a manner of right living that is a constant reflection of His glory and His holiness (see 1 Peter 1:14–16); in other words, a life of overcoming sin. His power is the only power that can make such living possible (see 1 Corinthians 2:5).

The sin that resides within every human being (see 1 John 1:8) is clever enough to allow for personal accomplishments that all too often lead to self-reliance and a denial of an internal sin presence. Material success, happiness, a moderate moral compass, a reasonable level of integrity, and/or lots of friends can all act as blinders to the true state of our inherited spiritual condition.

"The boastful pride of life" (1 John 2:16b) is a real tool that Satan uses to keep people from realizing his influence within them. Rather than holding ourselves accountable to God's standard of holy living, we subtly, and sometimes not so subtly, become worldly in our perspectives. We measure the rightness of the way we are living over and against our observation and assessment of the manner in which others are living.

All too often, we pat ourselves on the back, content that we are doing better than the next person. The absolute truth in this regard is this: the priority of life is not to be doing better than the next person; the priority

THE GOSPEL YOU'VE NEVER HEARD

of life is to be a consistent reflection of the glory and holiness of God!

The eleventh chapter of Hebrews reviews a history of individuals who by faith accomplished incredible things, and yet, even though they gained approval through their faith, they never received a release from their captivity to sin. They had to welcome the promise of the eventual freedom from that captivity "from a distance" (see Hebrews 11:13) because the Son of God had not yet come into the world.

Nevertheless, as unregenerate people, the Bible affirms that they lived their lives endeavoring to obey God, and, as a result, they were regarded as righteous in His eyes. This is an affirmation that though they were not "made righteous," they were reckoned, or considered, by God "as righteous" because they had "lived by faith." You can be certain that there were others who, though unnamed in Scripture, will be welcomed into an eternity with God for the same reason—they too will have endeavored to "live by faith."

Two thousand years ago, God provided something better for His human creation. By the sacrificial offering of His Son, He afforded mankind the opportunity to become regenerated into a new life of freedom and empowerment that would enable consistent holy living. The challenge to us all is: "How shall we escape if we neglect so great a salvation?" (Hebrews 2:3a).

85

Deliberations

Questions for Reflection or Group Study

1. Read 2 Timothy 4:3. What is it that Paul is warning will come? How might the idiom "have your cake and eat it too" be appropriate to Paul's warning about the accumulation of teachers in accordance with one's own desires?

2. How does Paul bookend his letter to the Romans? What do these common bookends suggest to us about the Gospel itself?

3. In your own words, describe what history has referred to as "the human condition." How does the Gospel illuminate the cause of this condition, and what does it offer as a solution?

4. Share or journal your thoughts on the reality of the spiritual presence of sin within you. Do you think the recognition of such a presence is common to most people? Why or why not?

5. The apostle John wrote of the difficulties that are brought on by what he called "the boastful pride of life" (see 1 John 2:15–17). If an invisible third party were to observe you over the course of the next week, what would they identify about your perspective regarding the value of the things of this life? If you can, share how you feel about the thought of such an evaluation.

7

Realizing Our Obligation

Paul begins Romans, chapter seven, with a short (six verses) "marital metaphor"[1] to further explain his "earlier references to believers' being set free from the reigns of death (6:9) and sin (6:14)."[2] Before we jump into those beginning verses, I want to share some additional teaching from the book of Job that will help us better understand Paul's use of the married woman and her husband and the metaphorical comparisons he makes.

Though Job is among the most well-known biblical characters, the message from the following Job verses is rarely taught. It is a message that explains the "law of God [concerning] the inner man" (Romans 7:22b), and it applies to every human being. Knowing and understanding this law is essential to the proper understanding of the gospel itself.

In the beginning chapters of Job, we read of a discussion between God and Satan regarding the righteousness of Job. From chapter one, verses 8–11, we read:

And the LORD said to Satan, "Have you considered My servant Job? For there is no one like him on the earth, a blameless and upright man, fearing God and turning away from evil." Then Satan answered the LORD, "Does Job fear God for nothing? Hast Thou not made a hedge about him and his house and all that he has, on every side? Thou hast blessed the work of his hands, and his possessions have increased in the land. But put forth Thy hand now and touch all that he has; he will surely curse Thee to Thy face."

Job 1: 8–11

In this passage, God draws attention to the righteousness of Job, and, in response, Satan makes an argument. He points out that Job's righteousness is not of his own doing but a result of God's protection from the difficulties of life and, therefore, is not to be regarded. Satan is so confident of Job's weakness apart from God that he boldly speaks of the assured outcome should God remove His protection: "But put forth Thy hand now and touch all that he has; he will surely curse Thee to Thy face" (Job 1:11).

It can be seen from God's response to Satan's challenge that this is not an argument without merit. God could have simply responded to Satan's charge by telling him that it was not for him to determine the justness of what He was or was not doing for Job. God is

God. He can do whatever He wants with whomever He chooses.

But that is not how God responded. "Then the LORD said to Satan, 'Behold all that he has is in your power, only do not put forth your hand on him'" (Job 1:12). Thus, by the allowance of God, Satan ravages Job's family and his possessions.

Satan was given his opportunity, and he made the most of it. He brought about the death of Job's children and destroyed all his possessions. But to Job's credit, "Through all this, Job did not sin nor did he blame God" (Job 1:22). Satan was undaunted, however, in his pursuit. "Skin for skin!" he exclaims, "Yes, all that a man has he will give for his life. However, put forth Thy hand, now, and touch his bone and his flesh; he will curse Thee to Thy face" (Job 2:4–5). Note here that by seeking permission, Satan is acknowledging his inability to do anything apart from the allowance of God.

The Argument Builds

Again, it is God who must allow these things to take place, and because the merits of the original argument are valid, He does. He responds, "Behold, he is in your power only spare his life" (Job 2:6). In the first instance, Satan was given power over the externals (his family and possessions) of Job's life. In the second, he was given power over Job's body, "his bone and his flesh" (Job 2:5).

Notice there is a restriction, "only spare his life" (Job 2:6b). This is not an admonition to avoid the physical death of Job. The Hebrew word here translated as "life" is *nephesh*. It refers to a man's inner being, the very life that was breathed into him from the nostrils of God. It is that "spirit in man" (Job 32:8a), the God-breathed spirit that "gives them understanding" (Job 32:8b) and "gives [them] life" (Job 33:4). It is the seat of our faculties of reason and understanding, the place of our conscience, and the source of our conclusions.

God did not relinquish His rights of ownership over the soul of Job, nor has He ever done so with the soul of anyone (see Ezekiel 18:4). As with Job, God maintains His ownership interest in the soul of every human being and with it exercises His sovereign right of protection.

He has allowed a sin presence to reside within the flesh of every human being and given it the right of power—through the Law—to hold the soul in bondage (more on this in the next chapter). However, God has never allowed Satan to alter a man's faculties of reason and understanding. To have done so would have taken away the merit of personal choice. Absent the ability to reason and then choose, Job could just as well have let the flip of a coin determine his responses.

The Freedom to Choose
Righteous recognition is warranted only as a person is given the opportunity to know and understand the good or the evil of his or her experience. In that knowl-

edge, mankind must then have the freedom to choose to follow and serve one or the other. Only on the basis of that choice, and that choice alone, can a person rightly be regarded as righteous.

Given that opportunity, should a right choice be made, Satan's argument in regard to Job is refuted. Righteous recognition is indeed warranted. The freedom and responsibility of choice is one of the foundational principles in the whole of the Job story. It will also be the foundational principle in the day of the just judgment of God.

Let's take another look at Job's story with an eye on how he consistently responded from the seat of his faculties of reason and understanding, the place of his God-protected conscience. It will help us understand the above point more clearly. As we do this, I encourage you to imagine this to be a contemporary event.

Such tragedies as these, though different in form and substance, are happening every day, all over the world, and without partiality. They are due to the existence of evil in the world and the power of sin within every human being. So, why does God allow them? As Job's story reveals, they are a necessary means to expose humanity to that which is the opposite of Him.

Remember, in just a single day, Job had suffered unimaginable loss. Gone were virtually all of his external possessions and, more incredibly, all of his children (see Job 1:13–19). Yet, as the Scripture tells us, "Through all this Job did not sin nor did he blame God" (v. 22).

On a subsequent day, Job is inflicted physically, literally from head to toe (2:7). Here again, "In all this Job did not sin with his lips" (v. 10).

And then it began. The relentless verbal assault I noted in the previous chapter. Job's wife and his three closest friends began their long discourse admonishing him to confess his transgressions so that his good fortune might be restored. Job holds fast his integrity, exclaiming to God, "According to Thy knowledge I am indeed not guilty; yet there is no deliverance from Thy hand" (10:7).

But eventually, by way of a response to his unyielding accusers, Job does make a mistake. He declares:

> How long will you [friends] torment me, and crush me with your words?
> These ten times you have insulted me, you are not ashamed to wrong me.
> Even if I have truly erred, my error lodges with me.
> If indeed you vaunt yourselves against me, and prove my disgrace to me,
> Know then that God has wronged me and closed His net around me.
>
> **Job 19:2–6**

Despite this retort, the criticism from his friends continues until finally, in chapter thirty-eight, God speaks. Take special notice of what He says: "Who is

THE GOSPEL YOU'VE NEVER HEARD

this that darkens counsel by words *without knowledge?"* (38:2, emphasis mine).

What God will eventually reveal is that Job had been right in one regard (see 42:8c) and wrong in another (see 38:2). Throughout the ordeal, Job had steadfastly defended his integrity, arguing he could confess no personal sin because he was not aware of any personal sin. In fact, God had affirmed that very thing in the beginning. Job had not been ruined for cause; he was not being punished for sinning. As noted earlier, God had clearly declared that He had been incited by the merits of Satan's argument to "ruin him [Job] without cause" (2:3c).

Where Job made his mistake was allowing himself to measure the justness of God based upon the circumstances of his life, a mistake many of us still make today. To be fair, Job was simply reflecting the understanding of the time: commit sin, be punished; live rightly, be blessed.

In point of fact, the circumstances of life (any person's life) have nothing to do with the justness of God. Herein lies the principal lesson of Job's story. For Job to declare that God had "wronged" him was speaking "words without knowledge." Job didn't understand because, as yet, he didn't have the appropriate background knowledge to understand. But once God spoke, Job recognized his error and responded: "Behold, I am insignificant; what can I reply to Thee? I lay my hand on

93

my mouth. Once I have spoken, and I will not answer. Even twice, and I will add no more" (40:3–5).

But Now My Eye Sees Thee

When God finally finishes His reproof of Job, Job replies with words that are as significant in their message as any in the whole of the Bible. He states:

> I know that Thou canst do all things, and that no purpose of Thine can be thwarted. Who is this that hides counsel without knowledge? Therefore I have declared that which I did not understand, things too wonderful for me, which I did not know. Hear, now, and I will speak; I will ask Thee, and do Thou instruct me. I have heard of Thee by the hearing of the ear; But now my eye sees Thee; Therefore, I retract, and I repent in dust and ashes.
>
> **Job 42:2–6**

Here is Job's revelation restated in brief: "Never again will I allow any circumstance of my life to quantify or define the justness of God. I now understand that it is impossible for God to be anything other than just. Henceforth, He will forever be my only instructor."

Had Job's inner self's ability to reason and understand been compromised, he would never have been able to respond to God as he did. Job heard the word of the Lord, reasoned it out, saw his error—he had spoken words "without knowledge" (38:2)—and repented (see Job 42:1–6). He responded to the revelation of God of his own free will because he was able to do so.

There is not much more history to be known of Job, but I am quite confident that never again would he have allowed the circumstances of his life to define the character of God. No matter what the future would bring (he was restored two-fold with family and possessions), Job would henceforth seek and rely only on the instruction of God, whatever its timing and however delivered. I can only imagine what kind of a witness he would be today, given the Bible and the indwelling presence of the Holy Spirit. It is not hard to understand why God had such a high regard for Job.

God had protected Job's inner self, just as He has the inner self of every human being, and for exactly the same reason: to preserve the ability to discern the difference between good and evil and to validate the personal responsibility of choice. This is the law or principle that was referenced in the previous chapter.

Whatever the living circumstance of any individual, there is some standard of measure, a law or set of laws, whether personally or communally established, that every individual applies to his or her life. He or she does this from the place of this inner self as a response to the law that emanates from the heart.

Anyone who is truly a person after God's own heart will know this relationship, this inner conscience interaction that alternately accuses or else defends the way he or she is choosing to live his or her life (see Romans 2:15). With this inner self-identity established, we can now look at the first verses in Romans, chapter seven, and better understand the analogy that Paul is making.

Understanding Paul's Analogy

Paul begins this critical teaching by reminding his readers "that the law has jurisdiction over a person as long as he lives" (Romans 7:1b). Why does Paul start here with such an obvious statement? Because he is preparing his readers to better understand the metaphorical comparison he is about to make.

He wants them to understand that where the law is concerned, what holds true in the realm of physical life also holds true in the realm of spiritual life. To help make the point, he cites a specific law as it relates to a married woman. It is cited from the Torah (see Deuteronomy 24:1–4), a part of the only Scriptures the early church had available, and therefore he knew it was a law that most would be familiar with:

> Or do you not know, brethren (for I am speaking to those who know the law), that the law has jurisdiction over a person as long as he lives? For the married woman is bound by law to her husband while he is living; but if her husband dies, she is released from the law concerning the husband. So then if, while her husband is living, she is joined to another man, she shall be called an adulterous;

THE GOSPEL YOU'VE NEVER HEARD

but if her husband dies, she is free from the law,
so that she is not an adulterous, though she is
joined to another man.

Romans 7:1–3

We should think of Paul's reference to the law here
as a reference to that which establishes a clear and au-
thoritative line between right and wrong. In this case,
under God-inspired, Moses-authored Jewish law, the
right of divorce belonged only to the husband. Therefore, a woman was bound to her husband, and there
was no way for her to end the relationship except in the
event of her husband's death. In that sense, as long as
he was alive, the law gave the husband an incontrovert-
ible right/power to hold the woman in the marriage
relationship.

Having referenced the authority of that law within
the familiar physical realm, Paul begins his metaphorical comparison to highlight the universal impact of law
within the spiritual realm. This is where an awareness
of the God-breathed, God-protected inner self, identified through Job's story and present in us all, becomes
important:

Therefore, my brethren, you also were made to
die to the Law through the body of Christ, that
you might be joined to another, to Him who was
raised from the dead, that we might bear fruit
for God. For while we were in the flesh, the sinful

97

passions, which were *aroused* by the Law, were at work in the members of our body to bear fruit for death. But now we have been released from the Law, having died to that by which we were bound, so that we serve in newness of the spirit and not in oldness of the letter.

Romans 7:4–6

The comparison is this: the woman represents the inner self, the God-breathed, God-protected inner spirit that is essentially the conscious life of every human being. The husband represents the sin presence that has co-existed with the inner self inside the body of every human being since the fall of Adam. By the judgment of God, that presence was the consequence of the garden transgression (see Romans 5:16b). It was that consequence that determined a life of conflict with and bondage to the power of indwelling sin.

Like the husband holding the wife in a marriage relationship, sin is able to hold the inner self of every human being in a relationship as well. It is a relationship of bonded servitude, that of a master and a slave, established through the power it derives from any law or "letter" that draws a definitive line between right and wrong.

This is the inherited "old self," the unregenerate condition of every human being, that is referenced by Paul in Romans, chapter six (see Romans 6:6). As long as the law, in this case, a law from the Torah, remained

THE GOSPEL YOU'VE NEVER HEARD

in force, bondage continued because the power that sin derived from the law (see 1 Corinthians 15:56b) was greater than any power known to man, except the power of God.

Even if the inner spiritual self had a desire to be joined to another, through the law, sin's right of maintaining bondage prevailed. Absent the death of the old self and the subsequent resurrection of a new self that is no longer under law, any change of the inner self would be impossible. Therefore, the bondage would legally continue.

Now the Good News

Fear not! For the person who has accepted Christ, the necessary death of the old self and the subsequent resurrection of the new has occurred. It is precisely what happened to the believers in Rome when they assented to the truth of the gospel. It is precisely what happens to anyone who makes a genuine confession of faith in Christ. By faith, we are "united with [Christ] in the likeness of His death" (Romans 6:5a) and *"in the likeness* of His resurrection" (Romans 6:5b).

This is an entirely spiritual event, and as a matter of spiritual reality, this is what happens: when we accept the Lord, our old self (our pre-Christ, unregenerate human condition) dies, "knowing this, that our old self was crucified with *Him,* that our body of sin might be done away with, that we should no longer be slaves to sin; for he who has died is freed from sin" (Romans 6:6–7).

Why was it necessary that our old self die? "That [we] might be joined to another [...] that we might bear fruit for God" (Romans 7:4b, d), and thus, "serve in newness of spirit and not in oldness of the letter" (Romans 7:6c). As long as we are being held captive by the indwelling presence of sin, it is impossible for us to be joined in a relationship of spiritual oneness with the Lord. We must first be spiritually released—sanctified or set apart—from that captivity.

As a result of Christ's sacrifice, the opportunity for a release from the bondage that had caused all human beings to "fall short of the glory of God" (Romans 3:23b) is now available. By a "circumcision made without hands" (Colossians 2:11a), the human spirit, which was impure because of its spiritual bondage to the sin in our flesh, was made pure "in the removal of the body of the flesh by the circumcision of Christ" (Colossians 2:11b). As the Hebrew writer put it, "For by one offering He has perfected for all time those who are sanctified" (Hebrews 10:14).

In this "newness of spirit" (Romans 7:6), it is now possible for anyone who is sincerely striving to be a true worshiper of God to be doing so not just in truth, through intellectual assent, but also in spirit. In the purity of a newly sanctified spirit, a believer can now be ushered into a relationship of spiritual oneness with the only One whose power is entirely sufficient to fulfill

THE GOSPEL YOU'VE NEVER HEARD

the required objective of obedient living (see Romans 16:26d). Such are the worshipers whom the Father had been and still is seeking, for "God is spirit, and those who worship Him must worship in *spirit* and truth" (John 4:24, emphasis mine).

Personal Obligation

It is important to understand the message of truth within these first few verses in Romans, chapter seven, because the described condition of spiritual bondage, the pre-Christ, unregenerate human condition, is the human condition into which all human beings are born, without exception and irrespective of personal awareness. The reality of this inherited human condition is not a matter of opinion; from God's perspective, it is a fact of truth that He Himself established. Just as true is the provision of God's Son as the only remedy for a condition that prevents the realization of what should be the greatest desire of every human heart, the keeping of His commandments (see 1 John 5:3).

Genuine faith in the Lord changes the spiritual condition of every believer. He or she has been set free from the internal bondage that had been his or her inherited reality. But the acceptance of that gracious gift of freedom is not the end of the story. In fact, as Paul will note in Romans 8:12, acceptance of the gift has created an obligation (more on this in the chapter "Requirement of the Law"). + opportunity + responsibility

101

Possession of the Holy Spirit, by itself, does not guarantee consistent obedient living; but it most certainly makes such living possible. It has now become a matter of learning how to live in, by, and through that Spirit, i.e., how to be "led by the Spirit" (see Romans 8:14). As you will read, it has now become a matter of personal obligation (Romans 8:12) and repetitive surrender (1 Corinthians 15:31b).

THE GOSPEL YOU'VE NEVER HEARD

Deliberations

Questions for Reflection or Group Study

1. Why does God allow Satan to have his way with Job? What do you think of the merits of Satan's argument? What was the ultimate lesson that Job learned through his ordeal? What "instruction of God" do we now have available that Job did not?

2. From a spiritual perspective, describe the "old self" that Paul referred to in Romans 6:6? As the only remedy for this condition, describe what happens when we surrender our life to Christ? Why was it necessary for the "old self" to die (see Romans 7:4)?

3. Read John 4:23–24. Reflect on the relationship that Jesus was foretelling in those verses, and Paul was identifying in the phrase, "so that we serve in newness of spirit and not in oldness of the letter" (7:6). From a spiritual perspective, what does faith in Christ make possible?

8

The Law Speaks

I have noted several times now that I quite agree with Sam Harris's observation that "we believe most of what we believe about the world because others have told us to." This seems to be truer in matters of faith than perhaps any other area. We know by the data that most don't spend much time in the Bible. Thus, it is typically the voices from pulpits that determine what people believe. More times than not, those voices go unchallenged. When my pulpit-derived gospel understanding started to fail me, my real journey of learning began.

At the start of my tutorial with the Lord, I had no idea that I would be led anywhere near controversy. But soon, I found myself in the heart of "the greatest and richest of all the apostolic works,"[1] wondering if I'd made a wrong turn. Apparently, verses 7–25 of Romans, chapter seven, have historically been "one of the most difficult and debated portions of the [Romans] book."[2] It was a debate with which I became quite familiar.

THE GOSPEL YOU'VE NEVER HEARD

What was Paul trying to communicate in these Romans, chapter seven verses that depict such conflict and internal struggle? Was it the ongoing struggle that *regenerate* born-again Christians were going to have to endure for as long as they lived? Or was it the pre-Christ struggle of an *unregenerate* person still held captive through the Law by the power of indwelling sin? There were additional aspects of the controversy that suggested other interpretive issues, but the core of this debate centered principally on the regenerate/unregenerate question.

I rolled up my sleeves, committed to two things: 1) a word-by-word examination of each verse, and 2) to be listening for the voice of the Lord at every step. I soon realized that I was not at this seventh chapter of Romans by accident. This was the exact place where the Lord began revealing to me an understanding that ultimately changed everything. I had cried to the Lord for discernment, lifted my voice for understanding, and, as promised, from "His mouth *come* knowledge and understanding" (see Proverbs 2:2b–3, 6b).

Romans, chapter seven, especially these verses, should be considered among the most important writing in the whole of the New Testament. Their truth is essential to a correct understanding of Romans, chapter eight, which is the heart of the "good news" message. Misinterpret this chapter, and we may misinterpret the true meaning and purpose of the gospel.

The centuries of disagreement that have plagued this chapter have not well-served the preaching of the gospel. As noted earlier, we seem to have overlooked the guidance that Paul put forth toward the end of this very letter:

> Now may the God who gives perseverance and encouragement grant you to be of the same mind with one another according to Christ Jesus; that with one accord you may with one voice glorify the God and Father of our Lord Jesus Christ.
>
> **15:5–6; see also 1 Corinthians 1:10**

Addressing the Confusion

Having identified in the first six verses of Romans, chapter seven, the cause for the history of our disobedience (sin/law/captivity), it would have been most natural for Paul to have continued right into Romans, chapter eight, with a description of the ministry of the remedy: the Holy Spirit. But Paul was very aware of the struggle that many (mostly his converted Jewish brethren) were having accepting the diminishing role of Law. Especially troubling for them was the fact that "letters engraved on stones" that had originally been given with glory were now fading away and being replaced by something with an even greater glory (see 2 Corinthians 3:7–11). He very purposely begins verse seven with a question that seemingly affirms this awareness. If, in fact, it was the Law that gave power to the sin that held

THE GOSPEL YOU'VE NEVER HEARD

us in bondage, "What shall we say then? Is the Law sin?" (Romans 7:7a).

Before we continue with Paul's response to this question, it will be helpful to first review something that he had written at an earlier point in the letter regarding the purpose of the Law. At verse nine of chapter three, he was concluding his review of the human history that had preceded the coming of Christ. He pulled no punches about what that history had validated. It was a history of repetitive human sinfulness, a period in which "both Jews and Greeks [were] all [shown to be] under sin [...] THERE [WAS] NONE RIGHTEOUS, NOT EVEN ONE; THERE [WAS] NONE WHO UNDER[STOOD]'" (Romans 3:9b–11a).

When Paul writes that there was "none righteous," he is not saying that there was none who had "gained [God's] approval through their faith" (Hebrews 11:39a). We have but to reread the eleventh chapter of Hebrews to learn of the many who had gained such approval because they had met the criterion that the gospel would later reveal; that is, they had "lived by faith."

More specifically, what Paul was affirming with his "all under sin" and "none righteous" remarks was that throughout this entire pre-Christ period, not one person had been able to escape their spiritual captivity to sin. Before Christ's life, death, and resurrection, such an escape was impossible. They were without the opportunity to invite the Holy Spirit to be a passenger in their car. The whole of humanity (even those who had gained approval through their faith) had remained in the unrighteous spiritual condition that had been their inheritance at birth; throughout the entire period, even the "righteous by faith" had remained unregenerate.

A Universal Impact

So, by what means was this universally continuing unregenerate condition confirmed over and over and over again? By the work of the law. Here's how:

> Now we know that whatever the Law says, it speaks to those who are under the Law, that every mouth may be closed, and all the world may become accountable to God; because by the works of the Law no flesh will be justified in His sight; for through the Law *comes* the knowledge of sin.
>
> **Romans 3:19–20**

First, notice the words, "For we know that whatever the Law says, it speaks to those who are under the Law, that every mouth may be closed, and all the world may become accountable to God" (v. 19). This verse is Paul's description of an effect that is universal ("every mouth [...] all the world") on all to whom the Law speaks. And how can it be so universal? Because whatever the Law says, it says to those who are under it, and the spiritual condition of those who are under the Law is exactly the same. The spiritual condition is universally inherited, and it is universally unregenerate.

THE GOSPEL YOU'VE NEVER HEARD

Paul's use of the word "law" here implies a universal application and impact, meaning that whatever the source of the Law's voice, when it spoke, it spoke to the whole of mankind and with the exact same result. The best understanding of Paul's use of the word "law" in the above Romans, chapter three verses is the more inclusive definition that emanates first from the law that was written in the hearts of all humanity.

As noted earlier, the impact of the Law has been subsequently expanded upon over time by the other means that God has used to increase its influence: (1) by His own hand, (2) by the Hebrew law, and the rest of the Scriptures, and (3) via the natural outgrowth from the conscience of human beings as they have experienced and attempted to define, or draw lines (laws) between the good and evil of life.

There is only one law that all human beings have been under from the beginning of time. It is the foundational law that was written in the hearts of all mankind from the moment of Adam's and Eve's first bites. That law can be clearly seen to have been utilized by the indwelling presence of sin to ensure that the thoughts of a man's heart (save for Noah) were "only evil continually" (Genesis 6:5b).

Fortunately, the evidence of sin's use of this law is not all contrary. History clearly substantiates the existence of well-established legal systems within many cultures and nations that preceded the Hebrew law. This confirms exactly what was noted by Eidsmoe: "if man is a created being, it is reasonable to assume that his Creator placed within him a knowledge of right and wrong that forms the basis for *Law*."[3]

Not Just What, but Where

Knowing the universal impact of the law, a second and equally important takeaway from these verses is found in these last words, "for through the Law *comes* the knowledge of sin." The word "knowledge" is translated from the Greek *epignosis*. The full and exact knowledge of sin includes more than just the knowing of what sin is (e.g., you shall not...), it also includes the much more important knowing of where sin is. In the remaining verses of chapter seven, Paul lays out for his readers how the Law did its work (its ministry) as God's designated "tutor to *lead us* to Christ, that we may be justified by faith" (Galatians 3:24).

If there is anything Paul made clear in Romans, chapter six, and the first six verses of Romans, chapter seven, it is that those who have embraced Christ as Lord and Savior have become "united with *Him* in the likeness of His death" (Romans 6:5a) and are therefore "not under law, but under grace" (Romans 6:14b). By the Lord's sacrifice, sin's right of power to hold a person in bondage and create a continuing ongoing struggle has not been partially done away with; it has been totally and completely annulled (see Hebrews 9:26).

Because Jesus stayed the course to the end of His earthly life, sin no longer has any right of control in the

THE GOSPEL YOU'VE NEVER HEARD

life of a genuinely born-again, regenerate believer (see Romans 6:14a). It is only the unregenerate who are still slaves and legally subject to the contrary influence of the power of sin, the ever-present passenger.

A brief word on what it means to be "not under law, but under grace." This is not a statement that suggests that believers are no longer required to be obedient to the law. In fact, as we will review in the next chapter, Paul makes it very clear that the reason God sent His Son into the world as an offering for sin was "in order that the requirement [obedience] of the Law might be fulfilled in us" (Romans 8:4a). The above phrase simply means that obedience to the law is no longer something that a believer should be trying to accomplish in his own strength. He must be learning how to surrender that task to the new passenger in his car, the Holy Spirit.

In other words, when the law says, "don't do this" or "don't do that," we can now realize that it is no longer speaking to us. It is not that we dismiss its intent or that we don't hear it because we do. But we now understand that it no longer speaks to us because we are no longer under it; the old self that was under it has died.

It now speaks to the only One who can actually fulfill its requirement. It speaks to the Life that has now become ours and that also stands ready to "give [that] life to [our] mortal bodies" (8:11b). Therefore, obedience can and should now be accepted as a fully realizable goal through the power of the indwelling Holy Spirit.

To be sure, though a believer's freedom has been fully realized, the presence of sin within a believer has not been eradicated. Sin has retained its internal place of residence in the flesh and, because of this, wants the believer to think he is still subject in some way to its power. Indeed, there is an internal battle that continues in the life of every believer (see Galatians 5:17), but we will see that it is a battle that is no longer ours to fight.

What needs to be understood, however, and seems to be so little taught is how to surrender that ongoing conflict to the indwelling presence of the Holy Spirit, the very Life that is now ours (see Galatians 5:16, 18, 25). This surrender should be the understood obligation (see Romans 8:12) and the day-to-day intention of every regenerate child of God.

The Law Shows Us Our Sin

Returning to continue from Romans 7:7, we find Paul beginning his explanation of the ministry of the Law with a specific reference to one of the Ten Commandments:

> What shall we say then? Is the Law sin? May it never be! On the contrary, I would not have come to know sin except through the Law; for I would not have known about coveting if the Law had not said, "YOU SHALL NOT COVET."
>
> **Romans 7:7**

THE GOSPEL YOU'VE NEVER HEARD

There are two similar words that appear within this verse. The first is "know," which is translated from the Greek word *ginosko*. The writers of the New Testament used it when the knowing they were referencing was a knowing that comes from "an active relation between the one who knows and the person or thing known."[4] It was a knowing gained through experience or through a perception of the senses.

The second, "known," is from the Greek word *oida* and references a knowing that was intellectual in nature, gained as a result of observation rather than experience. By way of example, picture a burning candle. The melting wax tells us that the flame is hot. That is *oida* knowing. You can also determine the flame is hot by touching it. That is *ginosko* knowing.

Unfortunately, in our English translations, we have rendered both words as if they communicated the same meaning, without distinction. As a result, on occasion, we have missed the writer's intended meaning of a verse or passage. In this case, Paul could have used *ginosko* in both instances. But he didn't. And there was a reason.

Look again at the latter part of verse seven, "for I would not have known [*oida*] about coveting if the Law had not said, 'YOU SHALL NOT COVET.'" The Law speaks, and from its communication, the hearer gains an intellectual understanding of the standard of God, the standard by which our conduct is to be measured. We gain a conscious awareness of the "what is" of sin. In this case, coveting is a sin.

113

The intellectual knowing of what sin is has become the possession of the person to whom the Law has spoken. And remember, the Law only speaks to the unregenerate person; regenerate people are no longer under the Law. They have died to it. But the knowing of the "what is" of sin is only the first of two sin aspects that the tutor (the Law) reveals.

The complete knowledge of sin also includes the knowing of where sin is. Look now at the middle part of verse seven, "I would not have come to know [*ginosko*] sin except through the Law." Paul is telling us in this verse that apart from the intellectual awareness of sin (seeing the flame), the person to whom it had spoken would never have gained the experiential knowing (touching the flame) of sin.

This is both an intellectual and spiritual process of awakening. The *oida* knowing, gained from what the Law has said, triggers an active slave/master relationship between the inner self and the sin that is within the person to whom the Law has spoken. Through the experience of that relationship, the person's knowledge of sin becomes full and exact.

Because of the *oida* knowing, he gains the *ginosko* knowing and learns of the presence of evil within himself. For what happens when the Law speaks? Sin takes the opportunity given to it through the commandment ("the power of sin is the Law" [1 Corinthians 15:56b]), and as it does, we become consciously aware of its presence within us (see Romans 7:5). Apart from the Law, sin

THE GOSPEL YOU'VE NEVER HEARD

is without power, and from a controlling standpoint, it is unable to exercise a conscious influence. Apart from the Law, sin is like a light bulb without access to electricity and sits as an unseen, unheard, unnoticed passenger in our car.

In that sense, the person was unencumbered by an awareness of spiritual conflict before the Law. He was living free of a written code of conduct. But when the Law came, transgression was defined, and sin became active. It began to "reign in [spiritual] death" (Romans 5:21b) from its God-allowed place of residence within all human beings.

As Paul had noted earlier in the letter, "And the Law came in that the transgression might increase" (Romans 5:20a), that the resulting increased internal conflict would lead the conflicted person to a very important discovery regarding his human condition. God knew that sin (from its internal place of residence) would seize its opportunity of power derived through the Law and, thus, create inner spiritual conflict. As a result, a person could become aware (through the conflict) of the internal presence and controlling power of sin.

As such, the person to whom the Law speaks has become dead in his trespasses and sins (see Ephesians 2:1), for that which was to result in life for him instead resulted in spiritual death (see Romans 7:10). This is why Paul referred elsewhere to the ministry of the Law as the ministry of death (see 2 Corinthians 3:7). "What shall we say then? Is the Law sin?" (Romans 7:7a). On the contrary, "the Law is holy and the commandment is holy and righteous and good" (Romans 7:12). Rather, it was sin that was shown to be sin by taking that which was good (the Law) and, through it, effecting the spiritual death of any person to whom it had spoken (see Romans 7:13).

The Camera of Paul's Mind

Today we are able to capture our experiences in the moment with high-definition electronic gadgets of all sorts, enabling us to go back and review the memories at any time, even seeing moments of the past exactly as they happened. Obviously, such was not the option in Paul's day. Nevertheless, using the camera of his mind, he vividly recreates the reality of the *ginosko* experience.

What thoughts had been produced as a result of what the Law said? Answer: "coveting of every kind" (Romans 7:8b). From where came the thoughts? Answer: from within (see Romans 7:8a). For what purpose did this happen? Answer: that we might know (*ginosko*) sin, i.e., we might sense or feel its presence within us (see Romans 7:7b). How was it that the law could work such a result? Answer: "For we know [*oida*] that the Law is spiritual" (Romans 7:14a), having been given by God and therefore it can only be truly and consistently fulfilled by those who have been freed in spirit.

However, the life of the person to whom the Law speaks has not yet been freed in spirit. He is still unregenerate, for he is still "of flesh, sold into bondage to sin" (Romans 7:14b). Drawing upon his memory of the struggle, Paul writes: "For that which I am doing, I do not understand; for I am not practicing what I *would* like to *do*, but I'm doing the very thing I hate" (Romans 7:15).

His synopsis is this: with his mind, he has recognized the rightness of the Law, and he desires to fulfill it as a matter of obedience. But as he endeavors to put his desire into practice, he observes that with his body, he is doing the very thing that is contrary to the wishes of his mind. He becomes confused in the experience. But, using his God-given, God-protected inner self, he reasons it through. He writes: "But if I do the very thing I do not wish *to do*, I agree with the Law, *confessing* that it is good. So now, no longer am I the one doing it, but the sin which indwells me" (Romans 7:16–17).

Now We Have a Standard of Measure

Typically, we all experience the psychological conflict of dos and don'ts at a very early age. You might say parents are life's first lawgivers. And unless those parents are explaining the cause of this internal conflict, we just assume it is normal. We do not even contemplate the cause. We just keep trying to get our own way.

With these verses, Paul is explaining this cause and effect at its highest level. The person to whom the Law has spoken now has a standard of measure, and he wishes to fulfill it, and this desire to fulfill it should not be overlooked. As a matter of his own choice, Paul genuinely wants to be obedient to the will of God. He does not want to covet. Still, he finds himself doing the very thing that he does not want to do.

In that observation, he affirms his ability to know and desire the good. But his failure to not covet affirms that his own desire is not enough because he is controlled from within by something else: the power of sin. So important is the understanding of the indwelling presence of sin that Paul explains the same principle over again. This time, he relates the reasoning that led to the recognition "that nothing good dwells in me, that is, in my flesh" (Romans 7:18a). He continues by saying, "for the wishing is present in me, but the doing of the good *is* not. For the good that I wish, I do not do; but I practice the very evil that I do not wish" (Romans 7:18b–19).

He has observed that he is able to wish for the good. He reasons that his inner being (that God-breathed inner self, described earlier) is not the source of the problem. Rather, as he attempts to live out the thoughts and wishes of his mind, he observes that he acts in contradiction to his own desires. Therefore, the "nothing good" that dwells in him must be in the flesh. "For," he says, looking again at Romans 7:19, "the good that I wish, I do not do; but I practice the very evil that I do not wish."

Again, the experience convinces him, "But if I am doing the very thing I do not wish, I am no longer doing it, but sin which dwells in me" (Romans 7:20). What is it that a person under the law has learned as a result of this encounter with its ministry? Paul continues, "I find then the principle that evil is present in me, the one who wishes to do good. For I joyfully concur with the law of God [concerning] the inner man" (Romans 7:21–22).

Through the experience of this conflict, the person under the Law becomes aware of the spiritual presence and power of evil within himself. And he joyfully affirms the law of God that has protected the inner self (see Job 2:6) and its ability to know good and evil, to recognize and desire the good over and against the recognized evil within him. Thus, from the depths of his inner being, or conscience, the person to whom the Law speaks is able to wish to do the good that the Law identifies; the good he intellectually (*oida*) knows.

Mission Accomplished

However, finding himself unable to perform the good that he wishes, he uses his God-protected faculties of reason to observe: "But I see a different law in the members of my body, waging war against the law of my mind, and making me a prisoner of the law of sin which is in my members" (Romans 7:23).

The Law has accomplished its purpose. The person to whom it has spoken has gained an understanding of not only what sin is but, more importantly, where sin is. He knows it is within him, that is, within his flesh.

From there, through the power given it by the Law, sin has taken control and spiritually killed him. It reigns in his life, and there is absolutely nothing he can do about it. Hard as he might try to break its hold, he cannot get free. And in the despair of such bondage, he cries out, "Wretched man that I am! Who will set me free from the body of this [spiritual] death?"[5]

As we learn from the psalmist, it was a cry that God would hear and to which He would eventually respond (see Psalms 102:18–22).

By the time of the writing of this letter, Paul's own living experience had developed and affirmed his answer to the question regarding such freedom. It is the most glorious knowledge anyone who truly fears God and desires to keep His commandments can ever possess. In the overflowing joy of his gospel understanding, Paul immediately exclaims, "Thanks be to God through Jesus Christ our Lord!" (Romans 7:25a). He knows it is through Christ and Christ alone (see Acts 4:12) that a person can be delivered from "the body of [that] death" (Romans 7:24b).

In summary, what is it that Paul had learned as a result of the internal conflict that he has just described? He tells us, "So then, on the one hand I myself with my mind am serving the law of God, but on the other, with my flesh the law of sin" (Romans 7:25b).

THE GOSPEL YOU'VE NEVER HEARD

There is no simpler picture painted in the whole of the Bible of the unregenerate human condition (the inheritance of every post-Adam human being) than the one that is painted by this verse. And it is this human condition that had been the cause of the history of disobedience that Paul had referenced earlier (see Romans 1:18–3:20).

In the beginning, God made man a living human being to be a God-breathed spirit that is housed inside a body made from the dust of the earth. But "by the transgression of the one [Adam]" (Romans 5:15b) "sin [had] entered into the world" and in that moment, "death [spiritual] through sin" (Romans 5:12a) began to reign (see Romans 5:14a, 21a).

In that moment, the human condition was altered. No longer was the God-breathed spirit of man residing alone within the man. As a consequence of the transgression, sin had been given a place of residence within the man (see condemnation, Romans 5:16b), and, though unperceived, it was the pervasive spiritual power from Adam until Moses (see Romans 5:12–14).

But through Moses, "the Law came in [was increased] that the transgression might increase" (Romans 5:20a) so that through the resulting increase in the conflict of conscience, the true child of God might learn that the thing that kept him from accomplishing the obedient desires of his heart was not an external influence but rather an internal presence and power that reigned in his life. Such is the universally inherited unregenerate

121

human condition, and it is precisely that human condition that God sent His Son to remedy: *"leading* to the obedience of faith; to the only wise God, through Jesus Christ, be the glory forever. Amen" (Romans 16:26c–27).

That's the glorious message of the gospel!

THE GOSPEL YOU'VE NEVER HEARD

Deliberations

Questions for Reflection or Group Study

1. Romans 7:7–25 is a description of internal conflict. How is that conflict triggered? What is the principal lesson to be learned from the conflict? Reflect on the difference between *oida* knowing and *ginosko* knowing.

2. Regenerate (born-again) humanity is "no longer under law, but under grace" (Romans 6:14b). Does that mean that born-again Christians need no longer concern themselves with living rightly before the Law? Describe the "death" from which regenerate human beings have been delivered?

3. Review Romans 7:7–25 again and describe in your own words how the Law did its work (its ministry) as God's designated "tutor to lead us to Christ" (Galatians 3:24).

4. What does Paul's exclamation "Thanks be to God through Jesus Christ our Lord!" affirm about his understanding? Can you relate to Paul's exuberance, and have you ever shared it with someone as a reality in your life?

123

9

No More Condemnation!

Now that we understand Paul's Romans, chapter seven description for what it is, a picture of the ministry of the Law, we are well-positioned to accurately understand Romans, chapter eight, a description of the ministry of the Spirit. Coming out of Romans, chapter seven, with a misunderstanding of Paul's writing, can foster a misguided entry into Romans, chapter eight, and a misunderstanding of what he wrote. For centuries there have been some in the church who have taught that what Paul was describing in the last nineteen verses of chapter seven was a regenerate (born-again) person's ongoing struggle with sin, suggesting "that the Christian, so long as he remains in this present life, remains in a real, though limited, sense a slave of sin, since he still has a fallen nature."[1]

There is nothing in the gospel of the Lord Jesus Christ that suggests that the inherited sin presence within every human being will ever be removed during a lifetime. It remains a real presence within our car and wishes to maintain its position of dominance. But to imply that a born-again person remains in any way a bonded slave of sin is a misrepresentation that suggests that Christ's redemptive sacrifice was not entirely sufficient with respect to its objective.

To the contrary, by the spiritual circumcision of Christ, a circumcision made without hands, the spirit of every believing human being has been entirely set apart (sanctified) from the flesh where indwelling sin resides (see Colossians 2:11). The sin presence is still very much a passenger in our car, but there are absolutely no remaining strands attached to the regenerate human spirit that must afford sin a continuing right of control, limited or otherwise.

By the sacrifice of Christ, the condemnation that once subjected every human being to the pervasive influence of internal sin and the subsequent master/slave bondage to that same sin has been made entirely null and void (see Hebrews 9:26b). The period of sin's right to reign in death is over. This is precisely what Jesus meant when from the cross He declared, "It is finished!" (John 19:30).

As Paul tells us in Romans, chapter eight, it is the sin remaining in the flesh that has now fallen under the condemnation of God (see Romans 8:3c). In Jewett's words from his *Romans: A Commentary*: "Christ's death brings an end to the 'whole epoch' of sin's domination, offering a new *possibility* of living according to the Spirit rather than the flesh"[2] (emphasis mine).

There Is Now No Condemnation

In his second letter to the Corinthians, Paul referred to the ministry of the law as the "ministry of death" (2 Corinthians 3:7). In that same passage, he also referred to it as the "ministry of condemnation" (2 Corinthians 3:9), condemnation to the captivity of sin that perpetuates the conflict that chapter seven of Paul's writing so vividly described.

As we have seen, regenerate human beings are no longer under law. By their acceptance of the "freely and graciously given"[3] gift of God's Son, they have been released from their inherited captivity to sin. They are now spiritually positioned to become beneficiaries of a new ministry brimming with potential for reflecting God's glory, the ministry of the Spirit (see 2 Corinthians 3:8–9). And it is not just a ministry that leads to an acceptable life; it is a ministry that can (and should) lead to a gloriously empowered life (see Romans 1:4; also 1 Corinthians 2:4–5).

Paul begins his description of that ministry with the gospel's greatest declaration, "There is therefore now no condemnation for those who are in Christ Jesus" (Romans 8:1). It is important to understand that this declaration has absolutely nothing to do with the Judgment Day disposition of any human soul. It is in no way forward-looking.

THE GOSPEL YOU'VE NEVER HEARD

Rather, it is the declaration of a "here and now" reality. The price that the Son of God paid for the redemption of mankind from their inherited condemnation, our spiritual captivity to sin, had been found acceptable. As Paul put it, "So then as through one transgression there resulted condemnation to all men, even so through one act of righteousness there resulted justification of life to all men" (Romans 5:18).

By comparing the consequence (condemnation) of the one act of Adam with the consequence (justification) of the one act of Christ, Paul is making clear that by His personal sacrifice, Jesus had validated, or justified, the purpose of the first four thousand years of human history. The reason that all had fallen short of the glory of God was now understandable.

However, the spiritual captivity that had made it impossible for anyone to attain the glory of God did not invalidate the value of that history. Yes, God had been calling all mankind to an objective—obedience—which they could never attain. But what the gospel made clear was that during those "times of ignorance," God had "overlooked" their disobedience (see Acts 17:30a) precisely because of their captive condition, a condition which He Himself had determined (more on this in the chapter "The Big Picture").

What could now be understood was that all that He had ever required during this period of spiritual captivity was that they steadfastly endeavor to "live by faith." There was a purpose to their living. It was to affirm

127

that no matter how great the human desire to be living rightly before God, from the moment of Adam's transgression, it was going to be an impossibility. Why? Because the power of sin is greater than the power of man.

In his unregenerate condition, man was never, in his own strength, going to be capable of attaining the righteousness of God. But, for the joy set before Him, though He was guilty of nothing, Christ endured the cross (see Hebrews 12:2b), in order that the previously-held captives might not only be set free but also empowered to finally be able to accomplish the will of God: to be consistently obedient in an environment that is entirely contrary to that objective.

More than Possession

Though there are many, there is one misconception regarding the gospel that has contributed to the decline of Christianity in America more than any other. I will introduce it here and expand on it in later chapters. There is a current gospel mantra that goes like this: "If you want a meaningful life, a better life, and an eternal life in heaven, then believing and receiving is all that's required."[4]

This implies that the only thing needed to be the beneficiary of what the mantra promises is the presence of Christ in your car. Nothing could be further from the truth. In fact, it is a perspective that has led Christians into the same error in understanding that entrapped the Jews in the time of Paul.

THE GOSPEL YOU'VE NEVER HEARD

Let me use Paul to explain. Paul's kinsmen had fallen trap to the thinking that their mere possession of the Law and the right of circumcision was what put them in right standing with God. Their thinking was wrong. Read what Paul wrote to them regarding such a perspective:

> But if you bear the name "Jew," and rely upon the Law, and boast in God, and know *His* will, and approve the things that are essential, being instructed out of the Law, and are confident that you yourself are a guide to the blind, a light to those who are in darkness, a corrector of the foolish, a teacher of the immature, having in the Law the embodiment of knowledge and of the truth, you, therefore, who teach another, do you not teach yourself? You who preach that one should not steal, do you steal? You who would say that one should not commit adultery, do you commit adultery? You who abhor idols, do you rob temples? You who boast in the Law, through your breaking the Law, do you dishonor God? For "THE NAME OF GOD IS BLASPHEMED AMONG THE GENTILES BECAUSE OF YOU," just as it is written. For indeed circumcision is of value, if you practice the Law; but if you're a transgressor of the Law, your circumcision has become uncircumcision. If therefore the uncircumcised man keeps the requirements of the Law, will not his uncircumcision be regarded

as circumcision? And will not he who is physically uncircumcised, if he keeps the Law, will he not judge you who though having the letter *of the Law* and circumcision are a transgressor of the Law? For he is not a Jew who is one outwardly; neither is circumcision that which is outward in the flesh. But he is a Jew who is one inwardly; and circumcision is that which is of the heart, by the Spirit, not by the letter; and his praise is not from men, but from God.

Romans 2:17–25

Paul's point is unmistakably clear. In God's bigger picture of things, a Jew is not a Jew because of his ethnicity, because of what he possesses (circumcision, the Law, etc.), nor even because of what he thinks of himself. A Jew is a Jew who is one inwardly, having received a "circumcision [...] of the heart, by the Spirit, not by the letter." He has embraced the truth of the Gospel and is no longer receiving his praise from men but from God.

I want to take a liberty here that I am sensitive to, but I do so because I believe it makes a necessary and true point. I've made some changes (as seen in italics) to Paul's above words of admonition to the Jews. You will notice a change in the target audience, but not in the point being made:

"But if you bear the name *Christian*, and rely upon the *Gospel*, and boast in *Christ*, and know His will, and approve the things that are essential, being instructed out

THE GOSPEL YOU'VE NEVER HEARD

of the *Gospel*, and are confident that you yourself are a guide to the blind, a light to those who are in darkness, a corrector of the foolish, a teacher of the immature, having in the *Gospel* the embodiment of knowledge and of the truth, you, therefore, who teach another, do you not teach yourself? You who teach that one should not steal, do you steal? You who say that one should not commit adultery, do you commit adultery? You who abhor idols, do you rob temples? You who boast in the *Gospel*, do you dishonor *Christ*? For the name of *Christ* is blasphemed among *non-Christians* because of you, just as it is written. For indeed, *sanctification* is of value if you practice the *Gospel*; but if you are a transgressor of the *Gospel*, your *sanctification* has become valueless."

There are many in the church today who have misunderstood the gospel, much in the same way that the Jews misunderstood the value and purpose of what they possessed. Jesus did what He did for a far greater reason than to just become a passenger in someone's car. Christians have no less of an obligation to live in the light of revealed truth than did human beings of any other time in history (more on this in the next chapter).

With or without the Law, with or without Jesus Christ in one's car, God is not a respecter of persons (see Acts 10:34–35; also Romans 2:11). In the end, the righteous judgment of God will be revealed in exactly the manner that Paul described:

131

> To those who by perseverance in doing good seek for glory and honor and immortality, eternal life; but to those who are selfishly ambitious and do not obey the truth, but obey unrighteousness, wrath and indignation.
>
> **Romans 2:7–8**

So then, the mystery that had been kept secret "for long ages past" was indeed manifested in and through the gospel of our Lord Jesus Christ. It was a two-fold mystery. First, as to the manner in which God will administer a justness that will be "suitable to the fulness of times, *that is*, the summing up of all things in Christ, things in the heavens and things upon the earth" (Ephesians 1:10), there can be no doubt.

Irrespective of the time period of a person's life, God will render to each person according to his deeds. He will reckon as righteous any person who has endeavored to live in accordance with the truth that he or she could have and therefore should have known during the course of his or her living. Whether it be the truth of God as revealed in creation, the truth of God as revealed through the Law and the nation of Israel, or the fullness of God's truth as it was revealed through His Son, the standard of God's righteous judgment will be absolutely the same: "BUT THE RIGHTEOUS *man* SHALL LIVE BY FAITH" (Romans 1:17b).

Second, as to the "summing up of all things in Christ, things in the heavens and things upon the earth," the

THE GOSPEL YOU'VE NEVER HEARD

purpose of the whole of the human experience has been revealed. From the beginning, God always desired to be one with His creation forever, but He would never presume such a relationship apart from His creation's choice. And, as we have already established from Job, that choice is only valid if made in the light of reason.

For each individual, life was always to be about discerning and choosing between good and evil. That is why God began the learning experience by exposing man to the knowledge of both. By placing the tree of the knowledge of good and evil in the garden and declaring it off-limits (establishing His first law), God empowered Satan (see 1 Corinthians 15:56b), and, as a result, the foundation for choice was established. Thus began the conflict, the conflict between the truth of God and the lies of the evil one.

But God has always been there, in the midst of the conflict, revealing some sufficient-enough-for-the-times measure of His knowledge. And in the light of that knowledge, any person could choose to rightly cover his nakedness for the necessary moment of living, and in so doing, gain the Father for the everlasting moment of eternity. Being with God in any moment, or for eternity, has never been about God's response to man, it has always been about man's response to God (see Romans 11:34–36).

For centuries mankind has been bemoaning the existence of evil, wondering how a loving God could have allowed such to be a part of the living experience. In the light of the gospel, we can now understand that the

133

good, the bad, or the indifference of any person's living experience has never been the purpose of his or her life. The primary value of life is not in the possession of life itself; it is in the opportunity it provides "to know God, or rather to be known by God" (Galatians 4:9a), and then to choose God.

Whatever the circumstances of a person's life, whatever the time or length of his or her living, it will all come down to the day "when, according to my gospel, God will judge the secrets of men through Christ Jesus" (Romans 2:16). It will have always been a matter of the human heart, which is exactly why the chronicler wrote: "For the eyes of the Lord move to and fro throughout the earth that He may strongly support those whose heart is completely His" (2 Chron. 16:9).

THE GOSPEL YOU'VE NEVER HEARD

Deliberations

Questions for Reflection or Group Study

1. Was the period of the right of sin to "reign in death" supposed to continue beyond the cross of Christ? What do you think Jesus meant when he declared, "It is finished!"?

2. What is your personal conviction regarding the presence of the power of sin within you? How would you describe it?

3. Consider your own allegorical car traveling through life. Who is in the car with you? What is the journey like? How often are you conscious of who is driving your car?

4. What was the trap of misunderstanding that plagued the Jews in the day of Christ? What is a similar trap of gospel misunderstanding into which many in today's church have fallen?

5. What is the primary value of life?

10

Requirement of the Law

Let's enhance our understanding by tying in a couple of instances in which Jesus foreshadowed the coming ministry of the Spirit that Paul described in Romans, chapter eight. When we look at John, chapter four, we see where Jesus, "being wearied from His journey" (4:6), stopped to refresh Himself at a well. It was on a parcel of land that had been given to Joseph by his father, Jacob, centuries earlier (see John 4:5–6). While He was there, a Samaritan woman came to draw water. Jesus engaged her in a discussion, saying the following:

> Woman, believe Me, an hour is coming when neither in this mountain, nor in Jerusalem, shall you worship the Father. You worship that which you do not know; we worship that which we know, for salvation is from the Jews. But an hour is coming, and now is, when the true worshippers shall worship the Father in spirit and truth; for such people the Father seeks to be his worshippers. God is

THE GOSPEL YOU'VE NEVER HEARD

spirit and those who worship Him must worship
in spirit and truth.

John 4:21–24

Jesus was foretelling what would soon be possible
for true worshipers of God as a result of His coming
sacrifice. God would no longer be worshiped in a moun-
tain, as was the practice of the Samaritans (see John
4:20), nor would He be worshipped in a temple, which
was the practice in Jerusalem. Henceforth, He would
be worshiped internally (see 1 Corinthians 6:19). As we
have learned, it was possible for spiritually dead human
beings, the unregenerate, to worship God and embrace
His righteous directives because of the God-protected
ability to discern good from evil. Thus, despite this spiritually dead condition, human beings could still determine that "the Law [was] holy, and the commandment
[was] holy and righteous and good" (Romans 7:12) and,
in response, seek to fulfill it.

However, because "the Law [was] spiritual" (Romans
7:14a) and unregenerate humanity was not—they were
being held as spiritual captives by the sin presence
within them—it was impossible for them to fulfill the
Law's requirements (see Romans 8:4a). While we were
"in the flesh," we simply could not, in spite of a genuine desire, please God (see Romans 8:8). But as we have
learned, faith in Christ changes the human condition
from fleshly to spiritual and makes the fulfillment of

137

the Law's requirement, consistent obedience, entirely possible.

Jesus Visits with Nicodemus

Chapter three of John's Gospel has the more widely known discussion that took place between Jesus and "a man of the Pharisees, named Nicodemus, a ruler of the Jews" (John 3:1). The concept of being born again as a necessary means of seeing or "enter[ing] into the kingdom of God" (see John 3:3b, 5b) is presented by Jesus. Jesus is not talking about some necessary event that must take place if a person is to survive Judgment Day and enter heaven. He is talking about a necessary event that must take place if we are to accomplish the goal of obedience and prove the will of God, the true and genuine worship of God, in the ordinary course of living (see Romans 12:1–2).

"That which is born of the flesh is flesh," Jesus continues, "and that which is born of the Spirit is spirit" (John 3:6). He is laying a foundation of understanding that foreshadows the necessary and beneficial result that will become available to all who will choose to believe in the purpose of His life, death, and resurrection. He had already declared that the kingdom of God was at hand (see Matthew 4:17). He knows that being "born of the Spirit" is the only means by which human beings can enter that spiritual kingdom.

With these remarks, He is foretelling the benefit of His coming sacrifice and the resulting ministry of the

Spirit. "Truly, truly, I say to you, an hour is coming and now is, when the dead [in Spirit] shall hear the voice of the Son of God; and those who hear shall live" (John 5:25). From a spiritual perspective, the whole of unregenerate humanity is dead. There is no escape from that death save responding to the knocking of the Lord at the door of the heart.

We Are Free to Surrender

As we return to Romans, chapter eight, remember these verses come from the mind and heart of Paul, who has already identified his information source: not according to man but through a revelation of Jesus Christ (see Galatians 1:11–12; Matthew 23:8). As such, it is God's truth, and it can and must be trusted! Paul had earlier asked the question, "How shall we who died to sin still live in it?" (Romans 6:2b). In other words, how shall someone who has been released from his spiritual captivity to the sin presence in his car still let that sin presence influence the way he drives his car? He shouldn't! Because of the presence and power of the Holy Spirit, the believer is free to surrender the driving of his car to that Spirit, and it is something he should be endeavoring to do every moment of every day.

Paul continues in Romans 8:12 with grammatical emphasis on being under obligation. He writes, "So then, brethren, we are under obligation, not to the flesh, to live according to the flesh" In Greek, he uses *opheiletes*, which is from the root *opheilo*. It means "to owe" or "to be indebted."[1] The significance of the identity of the "we" to whom this obligation of indebtedness belongs is very important. Nonbelievers are still in their unregenerate human condition and remain subject to the power of the sin presence within them. They have neither the obligation, though they may have the desire, nor the freedom, though they may yearn for it, nor the enabling power—Holy Spirit—to live any differently from how they have always lived. Believers, on the other hand, having accepted by faith the gift of freedom from their inherited spiritual death, have an entirely different choice and responsibility.

Perhaps more importantly, this newly-acquired freedom carries with it a severe and lasting consequence if it is not embraced by a believer as a new way of required living: "for if you [those who have accepted the gift] are living according to the flesh, you must [in Greek, *mello*, meaning "are destined" or "will certainly"][2] die" (Romans 8:13a).

Brace yourself. What you are about to read in the next few sentences will be a perspective of understanding that many leaders within the church community have never presented. Therefore, many within the church community have not had the opportunity to consider it. It is an understanding that is as accurate as any I have presented in this book and is not according to man but according to the gospel of Jesus Christ.

What future death is Paul referring to in the above Romans verse? First, let's consider Hebrews 9:27. It

THE GOSPEL YOU'VE NEVER HEARD

reads: "And inasmuch as it is appointed for men to die once and after this *comes* judgment." The death that the Hebrew writer was referring to in that verse is mortal death. However, with his verse, Paul is not referencing our mortal death, but rather a death that waits as a certain destiny for those who once having been saved from their death in their trespasses and sins, and despite such a great salvation (see Hebrews 2:3a), go on living according to the whim of their former master. It is a future death that the Bible refers to as the "second death" or the "lake of fire" (see Revelation 20:14–15; 21:8). It is the death from which the actuality of escape for anyone, even a believer, will not be revealed until the Day of Judgment.

Many members of the Christian community have a faulty understanding of this concept. What we have just read in the previous paragraph challenges a belief that many churches have been espousing for centuries: the certainty of a born-again believer's place in heaven. Even within this very letter, Paul writes that if a person confesses Jesus as Lord and believes in his heart that God raised Him from the dead, that person will be saved (see Romans 10:9). And indeed, such a person is saved, but the most critical question we must ask is: saved from what?

What about That Word "Saved"?

It is time for another word definition, a word whose meaning has been more misconstrued by the church than any other within the context of the gospel. It is the word "saved" (*sozo* in Greek) or its derivative "salvation" (*soteria*). From a nontheological perspective, there are numerous definitions of the word "save(d)." We find that it means "to rescue from danger or possible harm or loss" as well as "to prevent a goal."[3] As to "salvation," we find such meanings as, "act of saving from harm; the saving of somebody or something from harm, destruction, difficulty, or failure."[4]

From a theological perspective, we find the definition for "save(d)" is "to set free from the consequences of sin; to redeem."[5] As to "salvation," it is "the saving of the soul from sin and its consequences."[6] Without question, the most common understanding of "saved" within the modern church is one that reflects a deliverance from the eternal punishment of God. According to this definition, believers have no need to worry about hell; born-again Christians are assured of heaven. But is that consistent with what we have just read from Paul in Romans, chapter eight?

Whether from a theological perspective or otherwise, the words "save(d)" and "salvation" are intended to be simple and shared in their meaning. In essence, "save" means "to rescue," with "salvation" meaning "the act of rescuing." By simple definition, the words "save(d)" and/or "salvation," in and of themselves, do not presume to answer the "from what" question. As a result, many people have missed the essence of the rescue. The gospel of the Lord Jesus Christ has been mis-

THE GOSPEL YOU'VE NEVER HEARD

takenly presented as an eternal life insurance policy, and, consequently, people have been embracing it for the wrong reasons.

The initial salvation of the gospel of Christ is not about eternal security in heaven; rather, it is about being saved from an inherited spiritual captivity to the innate sin presence in our car. Thus, once saved, obedience can become more than just a desire as a matter of faith; it can become a pattern of consistently righteous living to the honor, praise, and glory of God.

That Second Death

The Bible states very clearly that Jesus will be returning a second time "for salvation without *reference to sin,* to those who eagerly await Him" (Hebrews 9:28b). Having taken care of the law of sin and death (see Romans 8:2b) at His first coming, there will be no need for Him to deal with it again.

Understanding the difference between salvation from the inherited spiritual death of post-Adam man and the second death yet to be revealed on the day of judgment is critical to a proper understanding of the gospel. There is a cliché phrase that has been a part of some church dogmas for quite some time: "once saved, always saved." It is a past tense statement that can only be applied to the first salvation because that is the only one that has been revealed so far.

In that sense, it is a true statement. Believers can be assured that though they may find themselves erring in

143

judgment, making poor choices, or falling back into sin at some future moment, it will never be because they have been snatched back into their former state of captivity to sin. Once invited in, the Holy Spirit will never leave, and thus, a believer cannot lose that first salvation and the resulting freedom from captivity.

By temptation, the old master can cause a believer to stumble (see James 3:2a) and/or willingly choose to fall back into his service. A pattern of willful choice, if continued by a believer, has a severe and lasting consequence (see Romans 8:13a; also Hebrews 10:26–29).

In his Gospel, Luke records a story told by Jesus regarding the necessary state of readiness as it relates to His second coming. The Lord speaks of servants/slaves who by their master had been put in charge of responsibilities during the master's absence (see Luke 12:42–48). The story reveals an undeniable obligation to be "faithful and sensible" (Luke 12:42a) with the responsibility the servants had been given and the severe consequence they will face (see Luke 12:46–48) if they choose to live without regard for their master's eventual return.

The Lord presents three different servant/slave profiles. The first one is fully aware of his master's will but lives without any regard for his eventual return, beating the slaves in his charge and openly living as a sluggard (see v. 45). Upon the master's return, he will be cut into pieces and placed with the unbelievers (see v. 46). The second also knows the will of his master but chooses not to be ready or to act in accord with that will (see v. 47). Upon his master's return, he shall receive many lashes. But the third slave does not know the will of his master, and though he "committed deeds worthy of flogging, will receive but few" (v. 48). The point of the story? When the Lord returns, He will clearly be dealing with people on the basis of how they lived in the light of what they knew to be true.

For Christians, it is how He concludes the story that is most important. It is a very well-known but little heeded phrase: "From everyone who has been given much shall much be required" (Luke 12:48b). There is absolutely nothing that has been given to any human being of greater significance than the gift of the indwelling presence of the power of God. And there is no expectation that the Master has of His servants that cannot be accomplished by His indwelling presence and power.

Sadly, many churches have failed to include this aspect of salvation in their teachings. As a result, many believers will be unprepared at the Lord's return. They have been taught that the mere profession of faith guarantees their admittance into heaven, and consequently, they will not have effectively yielded to the power of the Holy Spirit within them.

Rather, they will have continued to drive their car independently (and not necessarily intentionally), relying on themselves to withstand the power of sin. Absent the true understanding of their first salvation, they will not have recognized the meaning of the need to "die to self" (see Matthew 16:24–25; Mark 8:34–35; also, Luke 14:27). They will have made the same mistake made by Paul's Jewish brethren (see Romans 10:2–4), who believed it was by their right of circumcision and their possession of the Law that they obtained the righteousness of God (see Romans 2:17–29).

The real question here concerns blame. Who will the Lord find most responsible for this failure to understand? Will it be the person who sincerely believed what they were told, and as a result, prayed the prayer of acceptance, honestly believing that they now had what the Lord came to give them: the certainty of heaven? Or will it be the preacher who misled them, albeit because of his or her own misunderstanding?

Do those preachers really believe that it will be acceptable to suggest that any fallen person's original prayer must not have been genuine, and therefore, they were never really in possession of the Holy Spirit, or their faith wasn't really "true" faith? How many times have you heard that as a response to the fall of a Christian leader?

I am content knowing that it will be the Lord Himself who will rightly and perfectly answer those questions. I will also be eternally grateful to know and understand the true message of the gospel as taught to me by the Holy Spirit through the Word of God.

The Right to Become God's Children

Despite what many churches may have been teaching for centuries, the gospel of the Lord Jesus Christ and security in the day of judgment has never been about the mere possession of the spirit of God. Read carefully: "But as many as received Him, to them He gave the right [or power] to become children of God, *even* to those who believe in His name" (John 1:12).

That verse does not say that those who receive and believe in the Lord automatically become children of God. It says that those who receive and believe in Him are given the right or power "to become" children of God. The gospel was never intended to be just about having the Lord's power, it was always to be about learning how to live by that power (see Ephesians 3:20).

But it is important to understand that the reality of having our bodies walking in lockstep with the will of the Lord (which should be the desire of our hearts) is not something that happens automatically. When Paul wrote the following: "But if the Spirit of Him who raised Jesus from the dead dwells in you, He who raised Christ Jesus from the dead will also give life to your mortal bodies through His Spirit who indwells you" (Romans 8:11), he was not implying that such life-giving activity happens automatically.

If it did, then no truly born-again child of God would ever sin because we cannot be in sin and in Christ at the same time (1 John 3:5–6a). And if we have verbally acknowledged Jesus as Lord and affirmed our belief in His resurrection from the dead (see Romans 10:9), then we can be most certain that the "Spirit of Him who raised Jesus from the dead" does dwell in us. Even if we stumble, we should never let anyone challenge that reality. How we are living will never be about the reality of His presence within us; it will always be about the reality of our presence within Him.

It is the choice to allow His hands to guide ours on our steering wheel that will determine the outcome. It is the choices that believers will have made in the complete and total freedom that is now theirs: whether or not to follow the spirit of God (see Matthew 16:24–26), whether or not to abide in that Spirit (see 1 John 2:28), and whether or not to embrace consistent obedient living from one day to the next as their most ardently desired goal. It is not that the "desire [for] a better *country*, that is a heavenly one" (Hebrews 11:16a) is inappropriate. But in the here and now, it remains as a hope, not a reality.

The here and now reality is that in Christ, "God has provided something better for us" (Hebrews 11:40a). In Christ, there now exists not just the possibility of life but life in abundance (see John 10:10b). And because of that, we must always remember that:

> The one who says, "I have come to know Him," and does not keep His commandments, is a liar, and the truth is not in him; but whoever keeps His word, in him the love of God has truly been per-

THE GOSPEL YOU'VE NEVER HEARD

fected. By this we know that we are in Him: the one who says he abides in Him ought himself to walk in the same manner as He walked.

1 John 2:4–6

What then is the obligation of the born-again believer? Paul continues, from Romans 8:13b–14, "but if by the Spirit you are putting to death the deeds of the body, you will live. For all who are being led by the Spirit of God, these are sons of God." From a spiritual perspective, sin's right of control over the believer has been permanently annulled, and from the moment of our confession of faith, we were ushered out of our bondage to sin and into a new relationship, a position of spiritual oneness with the Spirit of our Creator.

However, this new relationship is not like the old one, "For you have not received a spirit of slavery leading to fear again, but you have received a Spirit of adoption as sons by which we cry out, 'Abba! Father!'" (Romans 8:15). We have not been ushered from one dominant master/slave relationship into another. Our new relationship is now one of a recurring and very personal choice of submission. Who will drive your car? Jesus will not arbitrarily take the steering wheel from us. We must recognize and embrace the need to give it to Him, and we must learn to do it every single day.

Look again at Romans, chapter eight, verses 3–4: God sent His Son as an offering for sin in order that the requirement of the Law, obedience, "might be fulfilled in us." The above "might be fulfilled" is what is called the subjunctive mood in Greek and, by definition, "makes an assertion about which there is some doubt, uncertainty or indefiniteness."[7] It implies an inherent contingency.

In English, it is often indicated by words such as "should," "might," or "may,"[8] which are used to insinuate possibility rather than certainty. There is nothing in the gospel that suggests that the arrival of the Holy Spirit as the third passenger in a regenerate person's car guarantees the eternal destiny of that car. Romans 8:14 does not read, "For all who have the Spirit of God, these are the sons of God"; it reads, "For all who are being led by the Spirit of God, these are the sons of God."

For centuries, many Christian churches have been erroneously selling an eternal life insurance policy in the name of the Lord Jesus Christ. Many people have been led to believe that the word "grace" implies God's extension of blanket immunity, and thus, they have been embracing the gospel only as a means of evading the fires of hell, not as a means of accomplishing a consistently obedient faith life.

In faith, they have accepted the gospel that has been presented to them. They have heard the knock (see Revelation 3:20), opened the car door, and the Spirit of the Lord entered, just as He promised He would. But not having the whole truth of the gospel, they have relegated the Lord to the passenger seat of their car, falsely comforted that His presence secures their place in heaven in the event of a fatal crash.

They have never understood, in the light of the freedom that is now theirs, the necessity of learning how to let the Holy Spirit become the GPS of their car. The only pair of hands on any person's steering wheel is his or her own. As much as a believer would rejoice to be able to turn the wheel over to the Lord as soon as He arrives, it doesn't work that way. What we have to learn to do is how to die to self, and how to do it daily. We have to learn to let the Lord's will become our will so that our hands are being moved by His strength, according to His will.

Paul emphasized this idea very clearly in a couple of places. Most succinctly, "I die daily" (1 Corinthians 15:31b). Not weekly, not quarterly, but every day! Elsewhere he said, "we *are* afflicted in every way, but not crushed; perplexed but not despairing [...] always carrying about in the body the dying of Jesus, that the life of Jesus also may be manifested in our body" (2 Corinthians 4:8–10). By uniting with the death of Christ, Paul knew that he gained the life of Christ, and it is the abundancy of that life that must always be manifested in his own life.

The Reality of Journey

I think the verse that sums it up the best is one Paul wrote in Galatians. I'll paraphrase it to our car analogy: "I have been crucified with Christ; and it is no longer

I who drive, but Christ drives in and through me; and the life I now live in my car I live by faith in the Son of God, who loved me, and delivered Himself up for me" (see Galatians 2:20). This is surrender. It requires the complete presentation of oneself to be "transformed by the renewing of your mind, that you may prove what the will of God is, that which is good and acceptable and perfect" (Romans 12:2).

And as regards God's perfect will and the reality of the manner of living that proves it, again, Paul paints a wonderful picture:

> And He gave some *as* apostles, and some *as* prophets, and some *as* evangelists, and some *as* pastors and teachers, for the equipping of the saints for the work of service, for the building up of the body of Christ; until we all attain to the unity of faith, and of the knowledge of the Son of God, to mature man, to the measure of the stature which belongs to the fulness of Christ. As a result, we are no longer to be children, tossed here and there by every wind of doctrine [...] but speaking the truth in love, we are to grow up in all *aspects* into Him, who is the head, *even* Christ, from whom the whole body, being fitted and held together by that which every joint supplies, according to the proper working of each individual part, causes growth of the body for the building up of itself in love.
>
> **Ephesians 4:11–16**

THE GOSPEL YOU'VE NEVER HEARD

The spiritual freedom that is realized when one embraces Jesus as Lord is immediate, but the "grow[ing] up in all *aspects* into Him" is a journey that is life-long and never-ending.

It will be both different and similar for each of us. But there most assuredly should be a consistency in our seeking, no matter where we are on the journey: "But seek first His kingdom and His righteousness, and all these things shall be added to you" (Matthew 6:33). The only place we can find what we seek is "in Him," and that is exactly where we must always strive to be.

A believer has the promise that the Lord "will never desert" nor "forsake" (see Joshua 1:5; Hebrews 13:5b) him, but he also has the warnings of consequence for failing to abide in the new relationship that God has engineered. From Jesus Himself we read:

> I am the true vine, and My Father is the vine dresser. Every branch in Me that does not bear fruit, He takes away; and every *branch* that bears fruit, He prunes it, that it may bear more fruit [...] Abide in Me, and I in you. As the branch cannot bear fruit of itself, unless it abides in the vine, so neither *can* you, unless you abide in me. I am the vine, you are the branches; he who abides in Me, and I in him, he bears much fruit; for apart from Me you can do nothing. If anyone does not abide in Me, he is thrown away as a branch, and dries

153

up; and they gather them, and cast them into the
fire, and they are burned.

John 15:1–6

The message here is clear. The above words of admonition from the Lord are directed at those branches
that are in Christ. By a confession of faith, they have
been set apart from their captivity to sin and grafted
into a relationship of oneness with the Vine (see Romans 11:17–18). Jesus most assuredly knows whether
or not someone is in Him, i.e., whether or not they are
attached to Him as a branch. This is not a misplaced
warning to those who think they are branches. It is a
warning to those who, because of their attachment to
Him, have the full potential for fruit-bearing.

Undoubtedly, this new relationship of Vine–branch
abiding is fragile, especially in the early going. So,
the Lord promises to be ever pruning the fruit-bearing branches, that they may bear even more fruit. Of
course, the old sin master is quite distressed about the
faith choice that has been made. And as such, he is totally committed (see 1 Peter 5:8–9) to keeping a former
slave from realizing the primary benefit and purpose
of this newly reborn condition. What better way to do
this than to promote a form of godliness that is blind
to the necessity of remaining in spiritual oneness with
the Vine?

Look again at verse two of the Romans, chapter
eight: "For the law of the Spirit of life in Christ Jesus

has set you free from the law of sin and death." The law of the Spirit is most definitely a law of freedom. But it is extremely important to notice that the law of the Spirit is not only a law of freedom; it is also a law "of life in Christ Jesus." If the benefits of the power that this new passenger, the Holy Spirit, makes available are to be fully realized from one day to the next, then the relationship of spiritual oneness with that new passenger must be maintained.

As believers, we must endeavor to spend the rest of our days learning how to remain in that Spirit if we are to consistently realize the God-intended benefit of our rebirth. Scripture is clear:

> Therefore, since we have so great a cloud of witnesses surrounding us, let us also lay aside every encumbrance, and the sin which so easily entangles us, and let us run with endurance the race that is set before us, fixing our eyes on Jesus, the author and perfecter of faith, who for the joy set before Him endured the cross, despising the shame, and has sat down at the right hand of the throne of God.
>
> **Hebrews 12:1–2**

Deliberations
Questions for Reflection or Group Study

1. Jesus declared the Kingdom of God to be at hand. He introduced the idea of being "born again" as the only means of entering that kingdom. Was He referencing the possibility of a here and now experience or only foretelling a future event? Why does an entrance into the "here and now" reality of the kingdom of God require a "born-again" experience?

2. Using Romans, chapter eight, explain Paul's use of the word "obligation" (v. 8) and to whom it applies. Does his use of that word sit well with you? Why or why not? What is the obligation to which Paul refers (see 8:12–14)?

3. Within the context of the gospel, what has been your understanding of the meaning of the word "saved"? Do you see the importance of the "from what" question? Do you agree that the "once saved, always saved" phrase has been misleading? Why or why not?
What is the difference between the way in which the Lord works within the life of a believer versus the way the old master (sin) worked prior to the Lord's arrival, i.e., does Jesus automatically take control or does He ask for you to surrender it to Him (see Romans 8:15)?

11

Relationship of Oneness

Remaining in a relationship of spiritual oneness with the Lord is not a matter of conjecture. Remaining should be verifiable in a believer's life through works. Here again, we have a word whose meaning has long been misunderstood within the context of the gospel. The approach to understanding its use correctly is very similar to the approach with the words "save(d)" or "salvation." Just as with "save(d)" or "salvation," we always ask, "saved from what?" So also, it is with "works." We should always ask, "Whose works?"

On several occasions in John's Gospel, Jesus spoke of works as a validation of the spiritual oneness He maintained with His Father as He lived His own life. He saw this relationship of oneness with His Father as the means by which He accomplished the vitally important objective of "work[ing] the works of Him who sent Me" (John 9:4a). In response to those who were challenging His identity as the Son of God, He said,

MAURIE DAIGNEAU

> If I do not do the works of My Father, do not believe Me; but if I do them, though you do not believe Me, believe the works, that you may know and understand that the Father is in Me, and I in the Father.
>
> **John 10:37–38**

A few chapters later, John recorded additional words of Jesus that validated this abiding relationship of spiritual oneness with the Father even more emphatically. These were the means by which the Father accomplished the works that the Son evidenced:

> Do you not believe that I am in the Father, and the Father is in Me? The words that I say to you I do not speak on My own initiative, but the Father abiding in Me does His works. Believe me that I am in the Father and the Father in me; otherwise believe on account of the works themselves.
>
> **John 14:10–11**

What Jesus was saying is this: "If you don't understand or believe what I am saying, then watch what I do. The works that you see Me doing give evidence that not only is the Father in Me, but I am in the Father." Previously Jesus had said, "But he who practices the truth comes to the light, that his deeds may be manifested as having been wrought in [worked by] God" (John 3:21). These deeds are works of the Father that are supposed

THE GOSPEL YOU'VE NEVER HEARD

to be readily evident in the life of a believer who practices the truth. They are the very works that Paul affirmed as the works "which God prepared beforehand, that [believers] should [note: subjunctive mood] walk in them" (Ephesians 2:10).

What we must understand about our relationship with the Lord is that it is not one of cause and effect. It is not a given that His presence in our lives will consequently cause us to "walk" in those "prepared beforehand" works. His presence will not automatically produce His works in our life (see Philippians 2:13). His influence on us is not dictatorial. Our daily surrender is required (1 Corinthians 15:31b). Again, we must not miss the significance of what the Lord meant when He said, "for apart from Me you can do nothing" (John 15:5). That is not a reference about His presence in our lives; it is a reference about the necessity of our unwavering presence in His.

Spiritual Oneness

What Jesus wanted His disciples to understand more than anything else was that the relationship of oneness that He enjoyed with the Father was a necessary relationship that was about to become their possibility as well. He explains this in John 14:16–20:

> I will ask the Father, and He will give you another Helper, that He may be with you forever; *that is* the Spirit of truth, whom the world cannot re-

ceive because it does not behold Him or know Him, *but* you know Him because He abides with you, and will be in you. I will not leave you as orphans; I will come to you. After a little while the world will behold Me no more; but you *will* behold Me; because I live you shall live also. In that day you shall know that I am in My Father, and you in Me, and I in you.

Jesus wanted His disciples to know that though He was about to leave the world, He would not be absent from them. Having been raised from the dead by the will of the Father, another Helper (Holy Spirit) would return to them. By that Spirit, they would also be raised from the death that had been their inheritance through Adam by the judgment of God (see Romans 5:12–19). "In that day" (see Acts 2:1–40), the day when the Holy Spirit would come to them and "cleanse [their spirits] from all unrighteousness" (see 1 John 1:9b), they would experience the spiritual oneness of which He had spoken.

The necessity of this spiritual oneness is no more poignantly expressed by Jesus than in a portion of the prayer He offered to the Father on behalf of His disciples just prior to His betrayal. This was a magnificent expression of His love for the disciples His Father had given Him. As He anticipated His imminent departure, His prayer reflected His hope of spiritual oneness not just for them, but for all who would believe in Him through their word:

THE GOSPEL YOU'VE NEVER HEARD

Sanctify them in the truth; Thy word is truth. As
Thou didst send Me into the world, I also have
sent them into the world. And for their sakes I
sanctify Myself, that they themselves also may
be sanctified in truth. I do not ask in behalf of
these alone, but for those also who believe in Me
through their word; that they may all be one; even
as Thou, Father, *art* in Me, and I in Thee, that they
also may be in Us; that the world may believe that
thou didst send Me. And the glory which thou
hast given Me I have given to them; that they may
be one, just as We are one; I in them, and Thou in
Me, that they may be perfected in unity, that the
world may know that Thou didst send Me, and
didst love them, even as Thou didst love Me.

John 17:17–23

Jesus was very specific with this prayer. It was about
a consistent display of the spiritual oneness that would
convince the world that He had been sent by His Father.
It was to be the kind of oneness that He and His Father
had exhibited. And the key to such a display is being
sanctified in truth. "Thy word is truth." Dallas Willard
was right. The failure on the part of many believers (and
their teachers) to recognize the importance of being in
the teachings of Christ is exactly what accounts for the
weakened effect of Christianity in the world today.

Our Relationship with the Spirit

Looking at the Lord's use of the word "works," it is easy to determine that He was speaking of the "works of the Father" because He identified them as such. When we look at Paul's reference in Ephesians 2:10, we can know that he is referring to the "works of the Father" because he identifies them as having been "prepared beforehand, that we should walk in them."

In the light of what we know from the gospel, apart from a relationship of spiritual oneness with the Holy Spirit, it is impossible for any person to accomplish the "works of the Father." Reiterating what was noted above, Jesus called it the bearing of fruit and was very specifically noting the importance of such oneness when He said, "I am the vine, and you are the branches; he who abides in Me, and I in him, he bears much fruit; for apart from Me you can do nothing" (John 15:5).

James, the Lord's brother, went so far as to write the following regarding the necessity of evidencing such "works" as a way of affirming the validity of one's faith:

> Even so faith, if it has no works, is dead, *being* by itself. But someone may *well* say, "You have faith, and I have works; show me your faith without the works, and I will show you my faith by my works." You believe that God is one. You do well; the demons also believe, and shudder. But are you willing to recognize, you foolish fellow, that faith without works is useless? Was not Abraham

THE GOSPEL YOU'VE NEVER HEARD

our father justified by works, when he offered up Isaac his son on the altar? You see that faith was working with his works, and as a result of the works, faith was perfected; and the Scripture was fulfilled which says, "AND ABRAHAM BELIEVED GOD, AND IT WAS RECKONED TO HIM AS RIGHTEOUSNESS," and he was called the friend of God. You see that a man is justified by works, and not by faith alone. And in the same way was not Rahab the harlot also justified by works, when she received the messengers and sent them out by another way? For just as the body without *the* spirit is dead, so also faith without works is dead.

James 2:17–26

Though neither Abraham nor Rahab were regenerate people, their actions or works validated the foundational principle of the gospel that the righteous person shall live by faith.

The content (what they could know and therefore believe) of Abraham's and Rahab's faith was different from the content of the faith that has been revealed in the gospel, the faith of which James was writing. Neither Abraham nor Rahab had received what was promised (see Hebrews 11:39b) because the time of Christ had not yet come. However, because they acted in accordance with what they did know to be true, they gained approval through their faith (see Hebrews 11:39a). They were reckoned or regarded as righteous by the Father.

163

They were not made righteous because they remained in their unregenerate human condition. That's because the Father had reserved something better for those who would be made perfect (regenerated) through faith in His beloved Son (see Hebrews 11:40).

Whose Works?

This writing of James is in complete harmony with the teachings of Jesus and the words of Paul in Ephesians 2:10. The necessary works that James is speaking of are the necessary works of the Father that validate the faith of those who say they are believers in Christ. They are the works of the Father that Christ evidenced, and they are the works that Paul said born-again believers should endeavor to walk in. Yet, misinterpretation and confusion regarding the relationship between salvation and works are due in large part to a failure to ask the necessary question: "Whose works?"

Two verses in Paul's writings have contributed to this confusion. One is from the Romans letter: "Where then is boasting? It is excluded. By what kind of law? Of works? No, but by a law of faith. For we maintain that a man is justified by faith apart from works of the Law" (Romans 3:27–28).

The other is from Ephesians 2 and reads: "For by grace you have been saved through faith; and that not of yourselves, *it is* the gift of God; not as a result of works, that no one should boast" (Ephesians 2:8–9).

THE GOSPEL YOU'VE NEVER HEARD

In the light of the gospel, we can see and understand exactly what Paul is saying in each of these verses. He is not contradicting any of the teachings of Jesus, nor is he in any way in disagreement with the writings of James or with what he would write in his very next Ephesians 2:10 verse: "For we are His workmanship, created in Christ Jesus for good works, which God prepared beforehand, that we should walk in them."

In the above instances, Paul's use of the word "works," which he clearly identified as "works of the Law" in Romans 3:27–28, is meant to reference the human effort that is extended by someone who agrees that the Law is good and, therefore, endeavors in his own strength to fulfill it. By itself, that is not a misplaced desire. But if four thousand years of human history have confirmed anything, it is that the best and sincerest of human efforts still leaves us woefully short of the glory of God.

Unfortunately, the sin presence in all human beings is clever enough to allow for the accomplishment of some law-defined goodness from time to time. Such accomplishments will often be misread as an affirmation of one's own righteousness. Self-accolades and personal sufficiency have prevented many from realizing and acknowledging the controlling presence of sin within them.

When Paul writes, "For by grace you have been saved through faith; and that not of yourselves, it is a gift of God; not as a result of works, that no one should boast," we can now understand what Paul is talking about. If the objective of consistent obedience is to be realized in this life, there is a needed salvation from the spiritual death that has been the inheritance of the whole of humanity (see Romans 5:12).

It is a salvation that has made possible a spiritual relationship of oneness with Christ Jesus for the purpose of walking in the good works that God prepared beforehand. It is the salvation that can come about only as a matter of faith. It does not come from human accomplishment measured against some divinely authored or humanly engineered set of laws. This is exactly what Paul meant when he wrote, "for if righteousness *comes* through the Law, then Christ died needlessly" (Galatians 2:21).

Driving Our Spiritual Car

As followers of the Lord Jesus Christ, we have an obligation to learn how to drive our car in a manner that reliably and consistently reflects God's glory. In order to accomplish that objective, we must actually learn how to let Him empower our driving. We must remember to "die to self" every day (see 1 Corinthians 15:31c). We must regularly examine ourselves to see that we are in the faith (see 2 Corinthians 13:5) and remember that we have been crucified with Christ. It is no longer we who should drive, but Christ who should be driving through us. We are to drive by faith in the Son of God, who loved us and delivered Himself up for us (see Galatians 2:20).

THE GOSPEL YOU'VE NEVER HEARD

We accept the reality of the continuing presence of sin and know full well that temptations in life will be common to all. But we also recognize that in each instance, we must continually seek the way of escape that the Lord has promised to faithfully provide (see 1 Corinthians 10:13). We acknowledge stumbling in our lives and embrace the Advocate whom we have before the Father when we do stumble (see 1 John 2:1b). We also accept that the indwelling Holy Spirit is able to keep us from stumbling (see Jude 24). We have but to learn how to be continuously in the Spirit to achieve that goal.

Therefore, we will drive with endurance the race that is set before us, fixing our eyes on Jesus, the author and perfecter of our faith (see Hebrews 12:1b–2a). Realizing that ours is a never-ending journey of learning and responding (see Proverbs 9:9), we accept the challenge of attaining the unity of faith and the knowledge of the Son of God. Then we will be mature people according to the measure of the stature that belongs to the fullness of Christ (see Ephesians 4:13).

We affirm the reality that by making the above manner of living the priority of our lives, we have no need to worry about falling short of the prize of the upward call of God in Christ Jesus (see Philippians 3:14). We joyfully welcome all that the Lord offers because we know that we are now living under a law of liberty (see James 1:25a) by which we are freely able (and obligated) to choose who will be the driving force of our car.

To paraphrase, "as for me and my car, I will choose the Lord!" (see Joshua 24:15c).

THE GOSPEL YOU'VE NEVER HEARD

Deliberations

Questions for Reflection or Group Study

1. Prior to this reading, when you heard the word "works" within the context of a gospel discussion, what were your thoughts? Do you see the importance of the question, "whose works"? So, whose works should the life of a true child of God be consistently reflecting?

2. How important is the relationship of oneness with Christ toward the accomplishment of the "works" objective? Doesn't the witness of Christ suggest that He never did anything apart from His relationship of oneness with His Father? From a spiritual perspective, where should children of God always strive to be? Discuss how that can be accomplished (see Hebrews 12:1–2).

3. What must we learn to do (and how often should we do it) if we are to realize the full benefit of the Lord's presence in our car from one day to the next (see 1 Corinthians 15:31; also 2 Corinthians 4:10; 13:5)?

12

What About Eternal Life?

The greatest possession any person can have is not just the possession of the knowledge of God but also the certain wisdom and understanding that emanates from it. In Proverbs, Solomon often wrote of the interrelationship of these traits and the importance of possessing them:

"How blessed is the man who finds wisdom, and the man who gains understanding. For its profit is better than the profit of silver, and its gain than fine gold" (Proverbs 3:13–14).

"The beginning of wisdom is: Acquire wisdom; and with all your acquiring, get understanding" (Proverbs 4:7).

In chapter three of this book, we saw that the gospel message, properly understood, serves as a prism, a clarifier of the true light, through which the kind intention of all God had purposed in His Son could be known and understood. Apart from the "Washing Clothes" understanding of the gospel, many of its teachings have been

THE GOSPEL YOU'VE NEVER HEARD

misunderstood, e.g., what it means to live by faith, what it means to be saved, what it means to be under obligation, and what it means to evidence faith by works. Add to this what it means to "have eternal life."

In his Colossians letter (1:19; 2:9), Paul made two references to the fullness of God. Both passages of Scripture affirm the same idea, that within His Son, God made all of Himself to dwell in bodily form. From a theological perspective, this denotes the "totality of Divine powers and attributes"[1] all being "at home in Christ."[2]

Whether it is grace (see 2 Timothy 2:1), righteousness (see 2 Corinthians 5:21), wisdom and knowledge (see Colossians 2:2–3), power (see Ephesians 1:18–20), or most importantly, eternal life (see Romans 6:23; 1 John 5:11; John 5:26), all of these attributes of God are referenced as being found in Christ Jesus. Thus, when the Holy Spirit enters a believer's life, so do all of these attributes of God.

Faith in Jesus makes all of the above attributes available to us in the here and now. In fact, this is precisely why Jesus did what He did so that we might experience the exact same spiritual oneness that He has always enjoyed with His Father. It is a quality of life (spiritual worship) that had previously only belonged to Him (see John 4:23–24). This recognition will be especially helpful as we look now at what it means to have eternal life.

171

Considering a Difficult Reality

Remember, we know there are (two) "salvations" within the context of the gospel: the first being realized by a confession of faith in the Lord Jesus Christ, and a second that remains uncertain until the Day of Judgment when it will be revealed. There are also two experiences of eternal life.

For many, as regards the concepts clarified in this book so far, this idea may be the most difficult to understand or even accept. Jesus has been marketed for so long as an eternal life-insurance salesman that many Christians have unsurprisingly filed their policy away somewhere for safe-keeping. For them, it is very hard to consider a different reality. If you are in that category, I encourage you to read on with an open mind and heart. Understanding the difference in these experiences of eternal life is critical. Therefore, we will rely on a heavy dose of biblical references to once again sit at the feet of the only One we are to call Teacher (see Matthew 23:8).

Let's think about the first of these two experiences of eternal life as the here and now, and the second as the eternal reward that remains, as yet, a hope (see Romans 8:24–25). The first experience of the eternal life attribute is realized when the Holy Spirit enters the life of a new believer. In Greek, it is *zoe*, which is "the absolute fulness of life [...] which belongs to God."[3] It is the abundant and eternal quality of life that Jesus said He came to give us (John 10:10b).

THE GOSPEL YOU'VE NEVER HEARD

The second experience of eternal life references the reward that the Judge, Jesus, will give to all those who will hear, "Well done, good and faithful slave [servant] [...] enter into the joy of your master" (Matthew 25:23). This is the judgment that Jesus was referring to when He said, "these will go away into eternal punishment, but the righteous into eternal life" (Matthew 25:46).

Looking at the Here and Now

Let's look at some additional biblical references through the lens of the "Washing Clothes" gospel we've been examining, beginning first with the here and now. In John 5:24, Jesus states, "Truly, truly, I say to you, he who hears My word, and believes Him who sent Me, has eternal life, and does not come into judgment, but has passed out of death into life." The first part of this verse, "Truly, truly, I say to you, he who hears My word, and believes in Him who sent Me, has eternal life," is affirming the absolute fullness of life (*zoe*) that a believer receives with the arrival of the Holy Spirit. In the very next chapter, Jesus reinforces the same truth: "Truly, truly, I say to you, he who believes has eternal life [in the here and now]" (John 6:47).

The middle part of the verse, "and does not come into judgment," simply assures the believers that they will not come into judgment for past sins. The apostle Paul wrote the same thing this way: "God was in Christ reconciling the world to Himself, not counting their trespasses against them" (2 Corinthians 5:19a). The last

173

phrase, "passed out of death into life," references the only salvation that has taken place so far, a believer's salvation from his inherited spiritual death into his newness "of life in Christ Jesus" (Romans 8:2). This verse is not a reference to the eternal reward aspect of eternal life because, as we have already identified, Jesus will not be awarding that until the day of judgment.

Another very important here and now verse that is often mistakenly understood as an eternal reward guarantee is, "My sheep hear my voice, and I know them, and they follow Me; and I give eternal life to them, and they shall never perish; and no one shall snatch them out of My hand" (John 10:27–28).

Note the "and I know them" part of this verse. This is the *ginosko* knowing that comes from "an active relation between the one who knows and the person or thing known."[4] It reflects an experiential spiritual knowing or "touching the flame" that exists between parties as a matter of mutual choice and surrender. It is very definitely the two-way relationship that Jesus was referencing earlier when He said: "I am the good shepherd; and I know My own, and My own know Me" (v. 14).

There is a familiar verse in Revelation 3:20 that is somewhat similar: "Behold, I stand at the door and knock; if anyone hears My voice and opens the door, I will come in to him." To this point, for the purpose of enhanced understanding, we could add "and give him the 'here and now' presence of eternal life in the process."

THE GOSPEL YOU'VE NEVER HEARD

Ultimately, toward the success of this *ginosko* relationship, it is not just the opening of the door that matters; it also involves the believer's response at the Spirit's arrival. True sheep hear His voice, but, more importantly, true sheep actually follow Him. Remember what many believers have done as a result of naively embracing an erroneous gospel? They have unintentionally relegated the Lord to the passenger seat of their car, falsely comforted that His mere presence has secured their place in heaven.

That kind of relationship is not the *ginosko* knowing of His sheep that the Lord is referencing in John, chapter ten, and, consequently, does not carry with it the "and they shall never perish" promise. The "and no one shall snatch them out of My hand" part of this verse simply affirms that at no time can the evil one arbitrarily pull us out of our spiritual oneness with the Lord. That is something Satan no longer has the right of power to do. He can certainly still tempt us, but he cannot remove the Holy Spirit from our car.

If we find ourselves in sin, it is either because we have succumbed to its temptation, have failed to seek the way of escape (1 Corinthians 10:13), or we have stumbled and retaken personal control of our steering wheel. We need to be advised that the Word of God tells us that a two-way relationship is entirely capable of keeping us from stumbling (see Jude 24), but a one-way relationship—relegation of the Holy Spirit to nothing more than passenger status—is void of such a promise.

175

Losing in Order to Gain

There is nowhere in Scripture that more clearly reveals the consequence of this one-way relationship than in Matthew, chapter seven. The Lord is speaking of the Day of Judgment and says the following:

> Not everyone who says to Me, "Lord, Lord," will enter the kingdom of heaven; but he who does the will of My Father who is in heaven. Many will say to Me on that day, "Lord, Lord, did we not prophesy in Your name, and in Your name cast out demons, and in Your name perform many miracles?" And then I will declare to them, "I never knew you; DEPART FROM ME, YOU WHO PRACTICE LAWLESSNESS."
>
> **Matthew 7:21–23**

Notice that the "depart from me" declaration that Jesus made was not because "you never knew Me," but rather, "I never knew [*ginosko*] you." It will be a very difficult moment for all those recounting the many things they had done in the name of Jesus even though all the while He was sitting in the passenger seat. They will have very genuinely been doing the things they will be recalling, and they will have been doing them in His name, but they will have been doing them in their own strength. They will undoubtedly evidence an *oida* (intellectual) knowing of the Lord, but, absent

THE GOSPEL YOU'VE NEVER HEARD

the *ginosko* (experiential) knowing, they will have never surrendered the wheel.

Living our lives in Christ is not about us doing things in His name. It is about learning to let Him do the works of His Father through us. Paul was reflecting on this very thing when he wrote: "For you have died and your life is hidden with Christ in God. When Christ, who is our life, is revealed, then you also will be revealed with Him in glory" (Colossians 3:3-4).

Regrettably, there will be many who will have never realized the necessity of surrendering their lives to the Lord. They will not have understood the idea of losing their lives for the sake of the Lord and the gospel in order to find true life (see Matthew 10:39; also Mark 8:35). Just as Jesus surrendered His own life so that believers might know Him, so should believers surrender their lives so that He might know them. If the evidence of today's church confirms anything, it is that there are far too many "Christians" still living their own lives and ignorantly doing it in the name of Jesus.

Unfortunately, there will be many believers who have failed to understand what Jesus meant when He said, "He who loves his life loses it; and he who hates his life in this world shall keep it to life eternal" (John 12:25). This verse is profound in its meaning and not to be overlooked. Read it again, this time with my insertions: "He who loves his life [in this world] loses it [in the next]; and he who hates his life in this world shall keep it to life eternal."

A Reward Not Yet Received

Regarding "life eternal" as a reward not yet received, the apostle Paul, when speaking of the "day of wrath and revelation of the righteous judgment of God" (Romans 2:5b), tells of rewards that will be given on that day "to every man according to his deeds." He says that to those who seek glory and honor and immortality by perseverance in doing good, the reward will be eternal life. To those who are selfishly ambitious and do not obey the truth but practice unrighteousness, the consequence will be wrath and indignation (see Romans 2:6–8). From a believer's viewpoint, it is important to be reminded that, in a nutshell, to be "persevering in doing good" essentially means to be examining yourself daily to make sure the Lord is driving your car.

We see that eternal life and wrath and indignation are contrasted as Judgment Day rewards and punishments based on the righteous judgment of God. They are exactly reflective of the words that Jesus spoke regarding eternal punishment and eternal life: "And these will go away into eternal punishment, but the righteous into eternal life" (Matthew 25:46). These are both outcomes that are reserved for the day of judgment (see Matthew 25:46).

In Romans, chapter eight, Paul affirms that the escape from the second death or the lake of fire was, as yet, a hope, not a fact in evidence. He refers to an inner groaning or longing that continues within those who have received the first fruits of the Spirit yet have not

THE GOSPEL YOU'VE NEVER HEARD

received *"our* adoption as sons, the redemption of our body" (Romans 8:23). Despite the Holy Spirit's arrival, our back-seat antagonist continues as a passenger in our car.

Paul refers to the redemption of our body in this way: "For in hope we have been saved,[5] but hope that is seen is not hope; for why does one also hope for what he sees? But if we hope for what we do not see, with perseverance we wait eagerly for it" (Romans 8:24–25). It is not futile for believers to have this hope, i.e., "the assurance of *things* hoped for, the conviction of things not seen" (Hebrews 11:1), but, as noted previously, it is very definitely a hope, not a fact that is already in evidence.

Pressing on Toward the Goal

Over and over again, Paul's writing affirms that he never regarded the eternal reward aspect of eternal life as a given during the here and now. In his Philippians letter, he wrote,

> Not that I have already obtained *it* [...] but I press on in order that I may lay hold of that for which also I was laid hold of by Christ Jesus [...] I press on toward the goal for the prize [life eternal] of the upward call of God in Christ Jesus.
>
> **Philippians 3:12, 14**

Paul had been "laid hold of" by the Lord in a very dramatic fashion (see Acts 9:11–19). There was nothing that he ever wrote that did not reflect his understanding of (1) the reason for which he was laid hold of by the Lord (see Acts 9:15–16); and (2) the obligation he knew he had to "press on" to the end, "lest possibly, after [he had] preached to others, [he himself] should be disqualified" (1 Corinthians 9:27b).

There can be no doubt that from the moment the scales "fell from his eyes" (Acts 9:18a), Paul realized that his life was no longer his to live. That is why he would later write, "I have been crucified with Christ; it is no longer I who live, but Christ lives in me" (Galatians 2:20a). And at the end of his last letter, written just before his death, he assertively wrote,

> I have fought the good fight, I have finished the course, I have kept the faith; in the future there is laid up for me the crown of righteousness [life eternal], which the Lord, the righteous Judge, will award to me on that day [day of judgment]; and not only to me, but also to all who have loved His appearing.
>
> **2 Timothy 4:7–8**

This perseverance in doing good as necessary to the receiving of eternal life is not unique to Paul. The writer of Hebrews put forth the same idea when he wrote, "And having been made perfect, He became to all those who *obey Him* the source of eternal salvation" (Hebrews 5:9, emphasis mine). And John the Baptist echoed a

THE GOSPEL YOU'VE NEVER HEARD

similar refrain: "He who believes in the Son has eternal life, but he who does not *obey the Son* shall not see life, but the wrath of God abides on him" (John 3:36, emphasis mine).

Looking more closely at this verse, we see that John the Baptist was referencing both the here and now and the future reward aspects of eternal life. To better understand this, look at these verses from 1 John 5:10–12:

> The one who believes in the Son of God has the witness in himself; the one who does not believe God has made Him a liar, because he has not believed in the witness that God has borne concerning His Son. And the witness is this, that God has given us eternal life, and this life is in His Son. He who has the Son has the life; he who does not have the Son of God does not have the life.

The apostle John writes, "And the witness is this, that God has given us eternal life, and this life is in His Son" (1 John 5:11). This echoes what he had previously written in his Gospel letter: "that whoever believes may *in Him* have eternal life" (John 3:15, emphasis mine). And from Jesus: "Truly, truly, I say to you, He who believes in Me has eternal life" (John 6:47). This affirms the indwelling here and now reality of eternal life.

Following the car analogy, John's words (and those of Jesus) state that anyone who believes in the Son of God has received, in the here and now, a new passenger, the Holy Spirit, who possesses an attribute of God that is eternal life ("and this life is in His Son"). With this insight in mind, we can understand the words of John the Baptist:

> He who believes in the Son has eternal life [in the here and now]; but he who does not obey the Son [in the here and now] shall not see life [as an eternal reward in the future], but the wrath of God remains on him.
>
> **John 3:36**

John's words confirm that by believing in Christ, we can have the presence of eternal life in the here and now. But, as noted previously, the Lord's presence in our lives does not ensure the consistency of obedience, which is the ultimate objective of the coming of Christ. This underscores the importance of surrender and of prioritizing the development of a personal relationship with the Lord. It is the kind of vibrant "living by faith" that should one day have us echoing the words of Paul as though they were our own: "It is no longer I who live, but Christ [who] lives in me" (Galatians 2:20). It is that life—His life—being lived in the here and now that ensures our future reward.

An Expression of Guarantee or of Possibility?

There is perhaps no more familiar verse in the whole of the Bible than John 3:16: "For God so loved the world

THE GOSPEL YOU'VE NEVER HEARD

that He gave His only begotten Son, that whoever believes in Him should [note: subjunctive mood] not perish, but have eternal life." Unfortunately, this verse has been frequently cited to affirm that simple belief is all that is required to receive the eternal reward aspect of eternal life. In the light of the "Washing Clothes" understanding of the gospel, it is easy to see that this verse is not an expression of guarantee, but rather of possibility, i.e., the possibility of experiencing eternal life both as a here-and-now reality as well as a future reward.

To better understand the true message of this verse, let's review some of the other references to the idea of "perishing." Paul made reference to "those who are perishing" three times in his Corinthian letters (1 Corinthians 1:18; 2 Corinthians 2:15; 4:3). In each instance, "those who are perishing" or those who are on "the path to destruction,"[6] are in their predicament because they consider the gospel to be "foolishness" (1 Corinthians 1:18), and are unable to "see [its] light" (2 Corinthians 4:3). Jesus painted a very clear picture of the "why" of this reality:

> And this is the judgment, that the light is come into the world, and men loved the darkness rather than the light; for their deeds were evil. For everyone who does evil hates the light, and does not come to the light, lest his deeds should be exposed.
>
> **John 3:19-20**

183

But Peter affirmed something that has been clear from the beginning. While referencing the coming "day of judgment and destruction of ungodly men" (2 Peter 3:7b), he recounts what he knows is and always has been the true desire of the Lord: "The Lord is not slow about His promise, as some count slowness, but is patient toward you, not wishing for any to perish but for all to come to repentance" (2 Peter 3:9). No doubt he was recalling these words of Ezekiel:

> "Do I have any pleasure in the death of the wicked," declares the Lord God, "rather than that he should turn from his ways and live?" [...] "For I have no pleasure in the death of anyone who dies," declares the Lord God. "Therefore, repent and live."
>
> **Ezekiel 18:23, 32**

The message of John 3:16 validates the above as the truest desire of God. It has never been His will that anyone should perish, not in the here and now, nor at the day of judgment. But the subjunctive "should" in this verse points to something in the future about which there is some uncertainty, and its use here must not be overlooked. In his first letter to Timothy, Paul affirmed that God "desires all men to be saved and to come to the knowledge [*epignosis*] of the truth" (1 Timothy 2:3–4). Take notice of the order of events in that verse. There can be no doubt that believing in Jesus is all that is required to be saved so as to receive the indwelling presence of eternal life in the here and now.

But that initial salvation is just the beginning, not the end. As believers, we are now in possession of the Spirit that "will guide us into all truth" (John 16:13a), and as such, we should steadfastly endeavor to come to that "knowledge of the truth" by presenting ourselves "to be transformed by the renewing of [our] mind, that [we] may prove what the will of God is, that which is good and acceptable and perfect" (Romans 12:2).

By faith, we have declared our allegiance to the Lord, and as such, we can be certain that the eternal life of God is now present within us. But it is important to understand that the reality of having our bodies walking in lockstep with the will of the Lord is not something that happens automatically. By writing the following: "But if the Spirit of Him who raised Jesus from the dead dwells in you, He who raised Christ Jesus from the dead will also give life to your mortal bodies through His Spirit who indwells you" (Romans 8:11), Paul was not implying that such life-giving activity happens automatically. If it did, no truly born-again child of God would ever sin because we cannot be in sin and in Christ at the same time (1 John 3:5–6a). Now that He has arrived, we must consistently choose to designate the Lord as the only driving force of our car.

If we have publicly acknowledged Jesus as Lord and affirmed our belief in His resurrection from the dead (see Romans 10:9), we can be most certain that the "Spirit of Him who raised Jesus from the dead" does dwell within us. The Lord is not going to keep His presence in your life a secret. Understand that it is not necessarily a validation by emotion. If you believe with your heart and confess with your mouth (see Romans 10:9–10), with or without fireworks, He is present within you.

Even if we stumble, rather, when we stumble, we should never let anyone challenge that reality. How we may be living in any given moment will never be about the reality of His presence within us; it will always be about the reality of our presence within Him; it will always be a matter of who is driving our car.

Jesus is not only the way and the truth; He is the life. It is His life being lived through us that offers the only means we have of consistently accomplishing our heavenly Father's desired day-to-day objective of obedience (see John 14:6). This is the reason that Paul wrote the following: "For the word of the cross is to those who are perishing foolishness, but to us who are being saved [no longer losing the daily battle], it is the power of God" (1 Corinthians 1:18).

Life Beyond Death?

Look at what Solomon once wrote on the subject of eternal life:

He has made everything appropriate in its time. He has also set eternity in their heart, yet so that

THE GOSPEL YOU'VE NEVER HEARD

man will not find out the work which God has done from the beginning even to the end [...] For who will bring him to see what will occur after him?

Ecclesiastes 3:11, 22b

With these words, Solomon was lamenting not just the question, "Is there life beyond death?" but also mankind's inability to discover the answer. The greatest joy in the revelation of the mystery that had long been hidden from Solomon and all the past ages and generations is that the question God had set from the beginning is finally answered: eternal life can be experienced both in the here and now and in the hereafter.

We are assured, "this is eternal life [in the here and now], that they may know [*ginosko*] Thee, the only true God, and Jesus Christ whom Thou hast sent" (John 17:3). And, though not seen in the here and now, it can be assuredly hoped for as an eternal reward, that is, "the crown of righteousness, which the Lord, the righteous judge, will award to me on that day [day of judgment]; and not only to me, but also to all who have loved His appearing" (see 2 Timothy 4:8).

What a day that will be!

Deliberations
Questions for Reflection or Group Study

1. How do you feel about this idea of two "eternal life" realities? How does this perspective relate to what you have been taught about eternal life?

2. Do you find the idea of two eternal life realities to be scripturally sound? Why or why not? Consider the people referenced in Matthew 7:21–23: what do you think their perspective was regarding the idea of eternal life? What is the forecasted outcome for them?

3. How do you feel about your life in this world? What does Jesus suggest your attitude should be (review John 12:25)? Why do you think He suggested such a thing? Should the living of life be principally about one's personal desires or those of a Higher Authority? Why?

4. What is the impact of the meaning of John 3:16 when you recognize the "should not perish" understanding? Does the presence of the Lord in a person's life guarantee anything about the way he or she will live from one day to the next?

5. Is it enough for a Christian to merely have access to the power of God, or is there something more that he or she must be learning to consistently do? Remember Paul, "it is no longer I who live, but Christ lives in me" (see Galatians 2:20).

13

The Big Picture

The apostle John once wrote that it was the Son of God who "has given us understanding in order that we might know Him [God] who is true" (1 John 5:20a). And the apostle Paul wrote that we could rest in that understanding because it represents the "true knowledge of God's mystery, *that is*, Christ *Himself*, in whom are hidden all the treasures of wisdom and knowledge" (Colossians 2:3).

Where did we come from? Who are we? Why are we here? How should we live? Where are we going? These most consequential questions of life can only be answered once the "treasures of wisdom and knowledge" are discovered. Such discovery takes place in the light of understanding that only Jesus can give us.

The Bible speaks quite plainly about a plan that emanated from the heart of God regarding a people whom He has chosen for His own inheritance (see Psalms 33:11–12). It is a plan that was formed long ago, and it is a plan that He has been fulfilling with perfect faithfulness (see Isaiah 25:1) from the moment of its first unveiling. The Bible even declares that it was by this predetermined plan that the Son of God would be "nailed to a cross by the hands of godless men and put [...] to death" (Acts 2:23). Why would God devise a plan that would require the sacrifice of His own Son?

To understand, we must look at an overview of that plan, a plan that offers a bigger picture of life. It is a picture of the supernatural (and currently invisible) life that overlays our earthly experience. It is the context within which everything we know and experience is happening and being measured. This overview is offered not as a means of validating the existence of God but rather as a means of providing deeper clarity on the long-sought-after answers to life's questions.

That First Revelatory Step

Let your imagination take you back to a time in eternity past when absolutely nothing existed, nothing except God. It was an existence that had no meaning. "What? Why not?" you may ask. Because there was nothing in existence to define Him, nothing to confirm that God even existed. It didn't matter if He was loving or full of hate, just or unjust, all-powerful or a weakling. Good, bad, or indifferent, nothing about God mattered. He was entirely alone, undefined by isolation.

He could just as well have not existed. But He did exist, and at some time in that eternity past, He deter-

THE GOSPEL YOU'VE NEVER HEARD

mined to take His first revelatory step, the bringing forth of His only begotten Son (see Psalms 2:7; Hebrews 1:5). It was a providential step that marked the beginning of time, space, and matter. Let's take a look at that beginning.

In his classic book *The 7 Habits of Highly Effective People*, the late Stephen Covey indicated that the habits or principles of which he wrote had their source in God.[1] One such recommended habit was to begin with the end in mind. Covey believed it to be a habit that was "based on the principle that all things are created twice. There's a mental or first creation, and a physical or second creation to all things."[2] In other words, first, there's the planning, and then there's the act of bringing the plan to fruition.

There is a passage in the very last book of the Bible that evidences the end at the beginning of the original plan of God. It tells of a new heaven and a new earth, a place where there will be no more death or mourning or crying or pain, a place where God Himself will dwell for all eternity with all those who will have overcome (see Revelation 21:1–7).

But what is it that those residents of God's eternal kingdom will have overcome? It is the contrary influence of the knowledge and power of evil (see 1 John 2:13–14). So why didn't God just begin with the end? Why didn't He just create His perfect utopia and populate it with whatever type of creatures He wished? Well, to have done so would have been in contradiction with two of His most important (and inseparable) character traits: His love and His justness.

The true value of love rests in the fact that it is freely given and freely received. Love that is coerced or pre-programmed apart from choice isn't love at all. We can only use the word "love" here, with any modicum of understanding, because God Himself is love (see 1 John 4:8) and because He first loved us (see 1 John 4:19). If the Bible story affirms anything, it is that God clearly desires to spend eternity with creatures who have freely chosen to love Him and not just casually, but wholeheartedly (see Deuteronomy 6:5; Matthew 22:37).

Regarding God's justness, I ask: what is just about populating an eternal kingdom with creatures that He put there simply because He could, moving them about like pawns on a chessboard? Such a creative action would have invalidated the necessity and value of free choice as the means of gaining eternity. If no choices are made, no justness is required.

From both a heavenly and earthly perspective, He made His creatures with the ability to know and to think, and thus, to make choices. And what was His expectation? "But the righteous will live by his faith" (Hab. 2:4b; see also Romans 1:17b), that is, his creatures will endeavor—during the time of their living—to live in the light of what they could have and, therefore, should have known to be a true revelation of their Creator.

Knowing What Is and What Isn't

There is nothing that exists that does not exist in exact accordance with the creative plan of God. Over the course of human history, people have been discovering the absolutes or laws of that plan. For example, Sir Isaac Newton's Third Law of Motion reads: "For every action there is an equal and opposite reaction." Further defined, it means:

> In every interaction, there is a pair of forces acting on the two interacting objects. The size of the force on the first object *equals* the size of the force on the second object. The direction of the force on the first object is *opposite* to the direction of the force on the second object. Forces always come in pairs—equal and opposite action-reaction force pairs.[1]

Within the realm of defining knowledge, a similar characteristic holds true: it is impossible to know what something is if we do not know what something isn't. It is impossible to know that a cup of coffee is hot if we don't already know what cold is. Yes, we may call the cup of coffee whatever we want to call it, but whatever we choose to call it will have no clear meaning without a known contrary reference.

At the onset of God's initial decision to reveal Himself was the problem of the knowledge of good and evil. There is no question that the Bible affirms that God is good (see Psalms 100:5; 136:1; Mark 10:18), but without an understanding of the meaning of evil, his angels nor we could know and understand the meaning of good. And if you were to consider the reality of good and evil as equal and opposite action-reaction pairs, the disparity between them and the resulting influence of both are the polar opposites of each other.

As incredibly magnificent as the goodness of God is, so equally heinous is the destruction that evil brings to bear virtually every day. But, of course, none of this was knowable until it was revealed. Thus, in order for God to be known as He is, it was essential for Him to create and reveal the knowledge of not only what He is (good) but also of what He is not (evil).

Humankind has forever struggled with the juxtaposition of the love of God with the existence of evil. The idea that God would in any way, shape, or form be involved with, let alone create, evil has been difficult to swallow. Yet the Bible states clearly that all things were created, "*both* in the heavens and on earth, visible and invisible, whether thrones or dominions or rulers or authorities—all things have been created through Him and for Him" (Colossians 1:16).

Earlier, to the Romans, Paul affirmed this same idea:

> For I am convinced that neither death, nor life, nor angels, nor principalities, nor things present, nor things to come, nor powers, nor height, nor depth, nor any other created thing, shall be able

THE GOSPEL YOU'VE NEVER HEARD

to separate us from the love of God, which is in
Christ Jesus our Lord.

Romans 8:38–39

Paul is referencing the necessary elements of knowledge, i.e., the "things," that God has created in order
that He might be known. He is not referencing the act
of sin as a creation of God in the above verses. Whether
it be "thrones or dominions or rulers or authorities"
or "principalities" or "powers," all were necessary cre-
ations toward the recognition of the line between good
and evil. However, it is important to note that the act of
sin itself is entirely the result of individual choice.

If the Bible validates anything regarding the knowledge of good and evil, it is that they are polar-opposites
in intention and can exert significant polar-opposite
influences (powers) on the thinking of both God's angelic and human creatures. Because God created both
His angelic and human creatures with the ability to retain and process knowledge, both were susceptible (by
design) to these influences. An awareness of the knowledge of good and evil will be at the heart of God's final
administration of justness, "*that is*, the summing up of
all things in Christ, things in the heavens and things
upon the earth" (Ephesians 1:10b).

An Angel Who Had It All

The Bible does not provide a lot of detail about the
earliest stage of God's plan. We know that there was a

created heavenly kingdom that both He and an angelic host inhabited. We know that there was one[2] among the angels who had been created with a special splendor. He had been made perfect, being "full of wisdom and perfect in beauty," and was by God's own choice "anointed" to be a guardian of His throne (see Ezekiel 28:12, 14).

From the moment of his creation, he had been found blameless until there arrived a time when unrighteousness was found in him (see Ezekiel 28:15b). Apparently corrupted by his own splendor and status (see Ezekiel 28:17), he determined that there was no need to be accountable to anyone but himself; he determined to "make [himself] like the Most High" (Isaiah 14:14b).

Under the influence of the knowledge of evil, this corrupted angel, Satan, had convinced himself that—though he was in the very presence of God—he could subvert the supreme authority of the Creator. And so, he sowed the seeds of rebellion, expanding his corruption to what the Bible indicates was "a third of the stars of heaven" (Revelation 12:4). A war in heaven resulted, and Satan and his followers were defeated and thrown out of heaven to the earth (see Revelation 12:7–9).

So, what does this event tell us about the character of God's first order of created beings? The fact that Satan was able to convince only a third of the stars of heaven to join him affirms their individual freedom of choice, along with some level of cognitive ability to recognize right from wrong, good from evil. It confirms

THE GOSPEL YOU'VE NEVER HEARD

that a knowable standard of measure regarding choice had been established.

So then, just how serious was this offense? What was to be the outcome of this incident? Was the consequence of this first-ever act of disobedience to be a mere relocation of residence for the offenders? What did the justness of God require? The angels were going to have to be very, very patient. The answers to these questions were going to remain hidden in a mystery for quite some time.

God Had More to Reveal

Additionally, why did the Creator of the universe deliver these offenders into the world of mankind? Why would He put such a contrarian influence, such a destructively cruel force, into a creation the whole of which He had so readily declared "good" (see Genesis 1:10, 12, 18, 25, and 31)? The entire universe was at His disposal. Why the earth? It was all done as a continuing revelation through His divine plan, a plan that He very definitely began with the end in mind. The apostle Peter wrote that the things of the gospel were "things into which angels long[ed] to look" (1 Peter 1:12b). Paul referred to such things as though they were being played out as a spectacle (from the Greek *theatron* [theatre]) to the world, both to angels and to men (see 1 Corinthians 4:9).

God had changed the venue. He transitioned to an alternate theater because He had much more to reveal.

197

The world of human beings was to become the main stage for the continuing revelation of the depth of His love and the impartiality of His justness. The principal player would be a Man who, for a little while, would be made lower than the angels (see Hebrews 2:9). And with the passing of time, it would become readily apparent that the earth as we know it today was never intended to be the final destination for anyone.

It was no accident that the first law ever given within the earthly realm of God's creation was the law regarding the tree of the knowledge of good and evil (see Genesis 2:16–17). It is the law that ultimately allows for the knowing of God, the knowing of what He is and what He is not. From the perspective of God's justness, it is the law that established the reality of conscience, i.e., the measure of choice: first in the heavens, and then on the earth.

God knew exactly what was going to happen as a result of His placement of this law in the garden. He knew that Satan was present in the garden, and He knew that Satan would use the power he was given through that law (see 1 Corinthians 15:56b) to usher sin and death, spiritual, not physical, into the human experience (see Romans 5:12–14).

More importantly, He knew that Adam and Eve would fall victim to the wiles of the serpent because they lacked the prerequisite knowing of good and evil, and, therefore, they lacked the ability to discern the rightness or wrongness of the serpent's counsel.

THE GOSPEL YOU'VE NEVER HEARD

Driven by a personal hubris to do all he could to undermine God's authority and establish his own, Satan had the motive to gain measurable and meaningful access into the world of mankind. And, just as He would later do in the case of Job, God opened the door for him. This time it was with a tree. From that moment forward, in accordance with the predetermined plan of God, the whole world would lie in the power of the evil one (see 1 John 5:19), as it still does.

The die was cast. The age of unregenerate humanity had begun. For the next four thousand years, Satan would have unfettered access to the human spirit, and his sole purpose was to convince the whole of humanity that there is no higher authority in life than the authority of self.

How despicable is Satan? He knows full well that there is no authority higher than the authority of God, yet he will maintain his chosen course until he is "thrown into the lake of fire and brimstone [...] [where he] will be tormented day and night forever and ever" (Revelation 20:10). By his own choice, Satan ignores the certainty of his own destiny. And his primary objective: to take as many with him as he can. Such is the nature of evil!

199

Deliberations
Questions for Reflection or Group Study

1. What is your reaction to the idea of God as a self-existent being (eternally existent, without beginning and without end)? Do you find it a difficult or easy concept to comprehend?

2. As it relates to the concept of justice, discuss the importance of choice. What is the ultimate choice that all human beings must make (see Romans 1:17b)?

3. Consider the impossibility of the knowing what something is without knowing what it isn't. How critical do you think the knowledge of good and evil will be at the time of God's final administration of justness?

4. Do you believe Scripture validates the existence of Satan? What seems to be the purpose of his here and now activity? Regarding his awareness of his eternal destiny, what is his principal objective?

14

The Bigger Picture

As I have already mentioned, Scripture is replete with counsel about the benefits of acquiring wisdom. Such counsel is never given without encouragement toward the ultimate objective of wisdom acquisition: "And with all your acquiring, get understanding" (Proverbs 4:7b). Inaccurate understandings lead to undesirable outcomes.

If we haven't correctly understood the directions we have been given, they can actually work against us. We run the risk of missing the narrow gate (Matthew 7:13–14). There are many who believe that people are free to determine their own truth, and it is largely this point of view that has fostered the laissez-faire, let-people-do-as-they-choose attitude to the living of life. What this view really evidences is a failure to understand the bigger picture of life.

This chapter's "bigger picture" narrative deserves stand-alone emphasis because of the picture it paints. It is a biblically painted picture of understanding that the Lord has been creating in my mind since He and I began our journey together. Whenever I need to recalibrate my bearings, I mentally step back from the picture, just far enough to be able to take it all in. And every time I do, I am reminded of just how faithful He has been to His promise. "Abide in my word," He said, "*then* you are truly disciples of mine; and you shall know the truth, and the truth shall make you free" (John 8:31b–32).

The balance of this chapter will highlight just a few of the bigger picture things that I'm most frequently reminded of during this reflective exercise. They are the understandings, the truths, that changed everything for me. The picture spans the landscape of humanity. There is no one who has ever lived, nor will ever live, who is not in the picture. I have given it a name. I call it "In the Light of the Gospel."

The Truest Value of Life

First and foremost, when I pause to rest "In the Light of the Gospel," I am reminded that the truest value of life is not life itself. Rather, the truest value of life (as noted earlier) is the opportunity it provides to know God and, much more importantly, to choose God.

In one sense, Solomon was right. Based upon his own experience of the inequities of life, he wrote: "behold, all is vanity and striving after wind" (Ecclesiastes 1:14b). Even today, contemporary author and biblical

THE GOSPEL YOU'VE NEVER HEARD

scholar Bart Erhman affirms this Solomon perspective regarding the merits of life as follows:

> Ecclesiastes has long been one of my favorite books of the Bible [...] the wisdom that Ecclesiastes imparts is not based on knowledge acquired by generations of wise thinkers; it is based on the observations of one [very smart] man as he considers life in all its aspects and the certainty of death [...] The key term here is *vanity*. All of life is vanity. It passes by quickly, and then is gone.[1]

No honest assessment at the time of Solomon could have concluded otherwise.

But, as you might expect, Solomon was also wrong because he lacked (as does Erhman) the bigger picture understanding that can only be found in the gospel. He wrote that "the earth remains forever" (Ecclesiastes 1:4b), suggesting that since the earth remains unchanged forever, then anything and everything that happens within the confines of the earth is all there is. But, "In the Light of the Gospel," we can know that the earth as it now exists will not last forever. It will eventually be replaced by a "new heaven and a new earth" (Revelation 21:1) that will be inhabited by "God Himself" (v. 3), and, lest we forget, it will also be inhabited by all those who will have overcome (see v. 7).

How will these overcomers be identified? Based on the plans created from His own heart, God will be

203

choosing for His eternal inheritance (see Psalms 33:11–12) a people who will have endeavored to "live by faith" (Romans 1:17b). That is to say, they will have steadfastly tried to live in accordance with what they could have and, therefore, should have known to be true as a result of the revelations He made available to them during the time of their living.

It will be that factor, and that factor alone, that will identify them as overcomers. We will all one day find ourselves standing in front of the only One who will know with exactness the way in which we endeavored to live our lives. And it will have been our choice.

In addition, with certainty and a great deal of comfort, we can know that the justness of God will not fail any whose lives may have been randomly cut short by the ugliness of the evil that so permeates the world (see 1 John 5:19b). But whatever the injustices in this life (and there are many), we can know that the Lord will disperse His final and unerring justness upon any and every human spirit which will have ever lived, and He will do so entirely without partiality (see Acts 10:34–35; also Romans 2:11). "And He shall wipe away every tear from their eyes; and there shall no longer be *any* death; there shall no longer be *any* mourning, or crying, or pain; the first things have passed away" (Revelation 21:4).

Made in His Image

Secondly, as I stand and consider His masterpiece, I can see that He made us in His image, with a unique

THE GOSPEL YOU'VE NEVER HEARD

ability to retain and process knowledge. We come into the world with an empty database. The knowledge we acquire and store determines how we think. How we think determines how we live (Proverbs 23:7).

From our Creator's perspective, there most definitely is a right and a wrong way to live. How do we know that? Because the first law He ever gave, the law of the knowledge of good and evil, was not just planted as a tree in the garden. It was also written and has continued to be written in the hearts of all human beings as the means to establish the interaction of conscience.

It is the awareness of that law that, at a minimum, creates the responsibility of personal choice in each and every human being. It is the reality of that law that influenced a myriad of cultures to create systems of laws that defined the difference between right and wrong as they understood it at the time. We know that there has always been something of God, some confirmation of Him as a higher authority, that has been and continues to be evident to all human beings, though some will have chosen to suppress it (see Romans 1:18–20).

When the journey of life as we know it now has ended, and the Lord has returned to administer His justness (see Ephesians 1:9–10), we can be certain that there will be a "crown of righteousness" ready to be awarded to all those who have "lived by faith," especially to those who have "loved His appearing" (2 Timothy 4:8c).

205

Not Just One, but Two

As I continue to examine the detail of the picture, I can see something that I otherwise would have never understood. I can see that from the very beginning, there were going to be "two nations" (Genesis 25:23) or "generations" (Psalms 102:18) of peoples on the earth. The first would be a generation of people who, by the transgression of one person (see Romans 5:12–16), would be universally condemned to a life of spiritual bondage to the indwelling presence and power of sin. And because the condition would be common to the whole of humanity, they would be considered as vessels that had been made for "common use" (9:21b).

And even though God was "willing to demonstrate His wrath and to make His power known" (v. 22a) by justifiably destroying the entire collection of those vessels (as was almost the case in the days of Noah), He instead "endured with much patience [those] vessels of wrath [that had been] prepared for destruction" (v. 22b). And why? So that at a time of His own choosing, He "might make known the riches of His glory upon vessels of mercy, which He prepared beforehand for glory" (v. 23).

How would the vessels of wrath be changed into vessels of mercy? They would be offered the opportunity to be spiritually regenerated into a relationship of oneness with the only life capable of consistently reflecting the glory of God—they would be offered the indwelling presence of the life of His only begotten Son.

The Older Will Serve the Younger

As I contemplate the outcome of the history of those first-born and common "vessels of wrath," I recognize that it can be summarized in one sentence: "for all have sinned and fall short of the glory of God" (Romans 3:23). Even the uniqueness of God's interaction with Abraham and his descendants, a specially selected segment of that generation, did not change the overarching narrative.

It is hard to argue with Erhman's assessment of the period:

> Page after page of the prophets' writings are filled with dire warnings about how God will inflict pain and suffering on his people for disobedience, whether through famine, drought, pestilence, economic hardship, and political upheavals, or, most commonly, through resounding military defeat. God brings disasters of all kinds, both to punish his people for their sin and to urge them to return to him. If they return, the pain will cease; if they don't, it will get worse.[2]

However, when understood from a gospel perspective, we realize that the narrative of God's interaction with the Israelites could not have reflected anything else. Think about the things they experienced, and yet they were repetitively disobedient. Why such a consistent outcome? Because God's direct interaction with them did not change the fact that the Israelites re-mained unregenerate.

From the perspective of an inner spiritual condition, they remained a part of that first generation of common vessels. Even though their hearts had been "wholly devoted to the Lord [their] God, to walk in His statutes and to keep His commandments" (1 Kings 8:61), that first generation of specially selected people fell short of what had been the call of God. And why? Because they were being held spiritually captive by the insurmountable power of sin.

A Relationship Reserved for One

It should be clearly understood that by no means did this unregenerate spiritual condition determine the eternal destiny of any within that generation. In fact, "In the Light of the Gospel," we can know, by a review of the history, that there were many from that generation who were called, many who were justified (regarded as righteous), and many who were glorified despite their spiritual condition, because they had steadfastly endeavored to "live by faith" (see Romans 8:30; also Hebrews 11).

But, and this should not be overlooked, though there were many who were visited by the spirit of God throughout that history (see, for example, Genesis 32:24–29; Exodus 31:3; Numbers 11:17, 25; Judges 14:6; Nehemiah 9:20; Micah 3:8; Haggai 2:5), there were none who were ever sanctified or "regenerated" into a relationship of spiritual oneness with that Spirit. That was a relationship that had been reserved for the Son of God. It was for Him and Him alone to be the firstborn of a new generation (see Romans 8:29).

God Unjust? May It Never Be!

Before we continue with this new generation, it is important to know and understand Paul's answer to an obvious question that arose as a response to his gospel preaching. Question: wasn't it unjust of God to call people to obedience that by His design they could never accomplish? Answer: "There is no injustice with God [...] May it never be!" (9:14).

God is free to do whatever He wants, to have mercy and compassion on whomever He wills (see Romans 9:15). And the manner in which He extends such mercy and compassion is not determined in any circumstance by the willing (thinking) or running (effort) of any man (see v. 16).

What Paul is stating here is that there is no part of the plan of God that mankind had anything to do with authoring. God drafted His plan, in its entirety, before His first creative act, which was the bringing forth of His only begotten Son (Colossians 1:15). And it was certainly His right as the potter to make two different vessels from the same lump of clay (Romans 9:21). But what must be understood is that there is nothing regarding the creation of the two generations, the two vessels, that predetermined their eternal destiny.

209

Everything about the plan of God is generic. It applies universally and without partiality to the whole of humanity. And this can be seen more clearly by no other means than in the manner by which the spiritual condition of the two vessels was to be determined.

Jewett was correct to note that with this section of Romans, chapter nine, Paul is reviewing the "divine purpose"[3] of God's plan, especially regarding the "how" of the spiritual conditions. Utilizing well-known events from Israel's history, Paul explains the reality of "two generations" as a part of God's original plan. He references the twins Esau and Jacob, who were born to Isaac by Rebekah. They are an allegorical reference to the unregenerate and regenerate human spiritual conditions, as Esau and Jacob respectfully (i.e., the two vessels or two generations).

Paul notes that the reality of these unregenerate/regenerate conditions, and how they would be established, was predetermined by God prior to the initial birth of either:

> For though *the twins* were not yet born, and had not done anything good or bad, in order that God's purpose according to *His* choice might stand, not because of [human] works, but because of Him who calls.
>
> **Romans 9:11**

THE GOSPEL YOU'VE NEVER HEARD

In other words, "in order that God's purpose according to *His* choice might stand," no characteristics of either human spiritual condition were assigned to or created in the unregenerate (Esau) or the regenerate (Jacob) while they were still in the womb.

Paul is telling us that neither of those conditions was the result of anything done, good or bad, prior to their respective entrances into the world. Why? Because during His planning process, it was God's choice, His prerogative, to determine that the two spiritual conditions would be realized in exactly the same way: they would both be the result of individual human choice.

Thus, by the predetermined plan of God, Adam's unregenerate condition, or his captivity to sin, occurred after his creation as a result of the choice he made to eat of the forbidden fruit. And likewise, the reality of spiritual regeneration, or being born again, is available only as a result of the choice a person makes to accept Jesus as Lord. Both conditions occur as a result of a free-choice response to the post-birth actions of God. In the first, the placing of the "don't eat" law in the garden; and in the second, the sending of His Son into the world.

But the Second Is Not Like the First

It is extremely important here to remember and understand something Paul had noted earlier about the two spiritual conditions. In Romans 5:15, he wrote that "the free gift [regeneration] is not like the transgression." The manner in which the second or regenerate condition is acquired is not like the manner in which the first or unregenerate condition was acquired. Though the unregenerate condition was the result of the disobedience of just one person (Adam), God determined that the consequence of that disobedience (spiritual death) would fall to the whole of humanity (see vv. 12–14).

By contrast, though the obedience of the One (Christ) resulted in the justification of life for the whole of humanity, God determined that the resulting gift of righteousness (regeneration) would not fall to everyone automatically. Again, by the predetermined plan of God, it is available only to those who choose to embrace Jesus as Lord (see Romans 5:12–21).

As noted above, in both instances, God provided the stimulus. In the first instance, the effect of man's choice was universal; in the second, the effect of the choice is individually applied. In neither case was the resulting condition predetermined as specific to any individual. It was always going to be about personal choices made in the light of available knowledge. There couldn't be a fairer definition of justness.

Lesson to Be Learned

There is an even finer point that I can understand as I look a little more intently at the picture. Paul tells us that the Lord's selfless act brought "justification of life to all men" (5:18). In other words, by His action, the life experience of that first generation was validated. It had a purpose. In fact, as Paul affirmed, the failure of this "older" unregenerate generation served the younger or "regenerate" generation (see Romans 9:12).

There was a lesson to be learned, and it was this: God had endured with much patience the vessels of wrath in order that they might have ample opportunity to seek and yet "fall short of the glory of God," and thereby discover their predicament.

Because of the contrary presence of sin within them, human beings were always going to be inclined toward self, toward believing that they could achieve the righteousness of God through their own strength. Thus, God both allowed and "overlooked [these] times of ignorance" (Acts 17:30a). He displayed His patience, I suspect, as a means of nullifying humanity's inevitable yet empty charge: "But you didn't give us enough time."

The truth? There would never have been enough time for mankind to attain the righteousness of God, in other words, to become regenerate by their own strength. For certain, they could strive to "live by faith" and thus be regarded as righteous, but they could never be made righteous by freeing themselves from their inherited sin master. They needed the time to discover the reality of their captivity and to subsequently cry out: "Wretched man that I am! Who will set me free from the body of this death?" (Romans 7:24).

There is only one power greater than the power of sin, and until God made that power available to human beings, there would be no new generation. But, just as the psalmist had forecasted, the time for a new generation did come:

> This will be written for the generation to come;
> That a people yet to be created may praise the Lord.
> For He looked down from His holy height;
> From heaven the Lord gazed upon the earth,
> To hear the groaning of the prisoner;
> To set free those who were doomed to death;
> That *men* may tell of the name of the Lord in Zion,
> And His praise in Jerusalem;
> When the peoples are gathered together,
> And the kingdoms, to serve the Lord.
>
> **Psalm 102:18–22**

The "generation to come" and "the people yet to be created" is a reference to regenerate humanity. The "groaning of the prisoner" is the groaning that emanates from "those who were doomed to [spiritual] death" by the very God who was looking down upon them. Vessels of wrath, unregenerate humanity, who had been prepared for destruction would be transformed into vessels of mercy, regenerate humanity. "Thanks be to God through Jesus Christ our Lord!" (Romans 7:25a).

From God's Perspective

Finally, I have often contemplated the length of the initial stand-alone unregenerate period and found solace in the words of Peter: "But do not let this one fact escape your notice [...] that with the Lord one day is as a thousand years, and a thousand years as one day" (2 Peter 3:8). Those words help us realize that time has always been in the determinative hands of God, and His measure has always been eternal in scope. Nevertheless, while we are still among the living, we should have no greater anticipation for anything than for the return of the Lord and the arrival of the Day of Judgment.

We should embrace that hope as a motivation for a daily endeavor to let the Spirit of the Lord live through us. It is His life we must constantly be endeavoring to reflect. By the time He returns, we may have been asleep for quite some time, but we can be certain that that day will eventually come. We can also have an equally high level of anticipation that there will be an administration of perfect justness. Imagine being able to watch a decision-making process that will be impervious to erroneous argument, literally a process without error. And it will apply to every human being who will have ever lived.

What a comfort!

Deliberations

Questions for Reflection or Group Study

1. Reread Psalm 102:18–22. Consider the identity of the "generation yet to come [...] a people yet to be created." To what generation is this a reference: unregenerate or regenerate? And when the peoples and the kingdoms are finally brought together, what will they be doing and why?

2. Paul tells us that the disobedience of Adam brought a consequence that fell to the whole of humanity. In contrast, he says the gift of righteousness (regeneration) that became available through the obedience of Jesus is different. What is different about it? Both Adam and Jesus made choices: Adam disobeyed; Jesus obeyed. What did Jesus have (see Isaiah 53:11b) that Adam did not have? Hint: TKoGaE

3. Take a moment to consider this bigger picture of life; step away in your mind and view it in its entirety. Then consider that it is the picture in which you currently exist! In the light of God's will for your life, what is your greatest opportunity?

15

How Should We Live?

Unless we have hardened our hearts against the existence of a higher authority, there is a question that rises above all others for people of faith: how should we live? There is no greater error in the preaching of the gospel than the one depicting Jesus as a seller of eternal life insurance. Our Lord freely gave up His life not to guarantee anyone a place in heaven, but rather to bring about "the obedience of faith" (Romans 1:5b; 16:26c) in the here and now.

God desires nothing less from His human creation than necessary obedience (see 1 Samuel 15:22–23) that is intended to lead to a life that reflects the full measure of His Son (see Ephesians 4:13). Toward that outcome, overcoming the contrary influence of the knowledge (and power) of evil is an essential goal in life. For four thousand years, people of all faiths were falling short of that goal (see Romans 3:23). This was not necessarily because they had ignored it as a matter of choice but because of their universal unregenerate condition.

Two thousand years ago, God sent His Son as a remedy for that unregenerate condition, and despite what many in today's church would have you think, God was not sending His Son into the world to waive the requirement of obedience and replace it with the guarantee of a place in heaven.

Neither was He doing it as a declaration of His sudden preference for any and all who would simply "believe and receive." Jesus was sent *"as an offering* for sin [...] in order that the requirement of the Law [obedience] might be fulfilled in us" (Romans 8:3b–4a). For the first time, people can now realize what should be the greatest desire of the human heart: to be consistently obedient to the will of their Creator!

This obedience has been the desire of our Creator from the beginning. Jesus couldn't have been any clearer when He said, "Therefore you are to be perfect, as our heavenly Father is perfect" (Matthew 5:48). And Peter echoed a similar instruction when he said that we are to be just like the Holy One who called us: we are to be holy in all our behavior (see 1 Peter 1:14–16; see also Leviticus 19:2).

Living Our Lives Based on Scripture

How do we usually react to the idea of perfection or, more explicitly, holy living? Most of us, including me for a good portion of my life, think such a manner of

THE GOSPEL YOU'VE NEVER HEARD

living is entirely unattainable. Anyone who even suggests such is simply ignoring the realities of life. Here's
the problem with that perspective: true children of God
are not supposed to be living their lives based upon the
realities of life; they are supposed to be living their lives
based upon the instruction of Scripture!

So, how is it that Scripture instructs us toward the
consistent accomplishment of the Lord's mandate?
What is to be our understanding about His stated objective of perfect (holy) living? As I noted earlier, it has
been my hope that this book would present the study
that considerably changed my understanding of the
gospel. What I now know to be true regarding the gospel of the Lord Jesus Christ is entirely different from
what I first heard and embraced.

The light bulb started to go on for me when I first began hearing the Lord say to me: "Maurie, you must understand that I did not do what I did just to be the Lord
of your life. I did what I did to actually become your life!
It is only as you learn to let Me be your life that you will
be enabled to accomplish the will of our Father." I am
not ashamed to admit that I was flooded with emotion
as I repeated those words over and over in my mind. *He
came to become my life...He came to become my life.*

In an instant, many of the verses that I had read
so many times before began to echo within my mind
and heart. It was as though I was hearing them for the
first time. There are so many that it would take another
book to share them all, but in the remaining pages of

219

this chapter, I present just a few that most clearly affirm what I now hear every time I read them.

No Longer I, but Christ

> I have been crucified with Christ; and it is no longer I who live, but Christ lives in me; and the *life* which I now live in the flesh I live by faith in the Son of God, who loved me, and delivered Himself up for me.
>
> **Galatians 2:20**

> Or do you not know that your body is a temple of the Holy Spirit who is in you, whom you have from God, and that you are not your own? For you have been bought with a price: therefore glorify God in your body.
>
> **1 Corinthians 6:19–20**

> Test yourselves *to see* if you are in the faith; examine yourselves! Or do you not recognize this about yourselves, that Jesus Christ is in you—unless indeed you fail the test?
>
> **2 Corinthians 13:5**

Every day I have a choice: am I going to do my own thing, independent of anything or anyone, or am I going to let the Lord do His thing through me? We wake up in the morning with another day to live; we think

THE GOSPEL YOU'VE NEVER HEARD

we should immediately start planning and/or worrying about the necessities of life. No, no, and no! What should be the priority for that day and every day? "But seek first His kingdom and His righteousness..." (Matthew 6:33a).

The kingdom of God is a spiritual kingdom. The moment we accept Christ, we are transferred into that kingdom, introduced into the grace of spiritual oneness with the Lord Himself (see Romans 5:2). It is what we do with that introduction going forward that becomes the heart of the matter. These are not just words.

And it is not just His kingdom that we should seek to be in, it is also His righteousness. The only place we can find His righteousness is in Him. A true child of God will endeavor to spend the balance of his or her life learning how to live in Christ, or rather, learning how to let Christ be his or her life. We are to be patient and never give up. The Scriptures will guide us.

Treasure in Earthen Vessels

> Therefore do not be anxious for tomorrow; for tomorrow will care for itself. *Each* day has enough trouble of its own.
>
> **Matthew 6:34**

> But we have this treasure in earthen vessels, that the surpassing greatness of the power may be of God and not from ourselves; *we are* afflicted in

every way, but not crushed; perplexed, but not despairing [...] always carrying about in the body the dying of Jesus, that the life of Jesus also may be manifested in our body. For we who live are constantly being delivered over to death for Jesus' sake, that the life of Jesus also may be manifested in our mortal flesh.

2 Corinthians 4:7–11

For not one of us lives for himself, and not one dies for himself; for if we live, we live for the Lord, or if we die, we die for the Lord; therefore, whether we live or die, we are the Lord's.

Romans 14:7–8

If anxiety regarding the necessities of life is not to be our first focus of every day, then what should be our focus? From one day to the next, the priority of our focus should be on overcoming the trouble, the contrary influence of evil, that each day contains. And it is never to be about the accomplishment of doing that, about stringing as many perfect days together as we can. The minute we start doing that, we have started down the wrong path (see 1 Corinthians 10:12).

We need to hold ourselves accountable for how we live each of our days. We must be living for Him and not ourselves. When that day is over, praise Him for the joy of the day (and there will be moments of joy beyond measure) or seek His forgiveness if necessary. No one

THE GOSPEL YOU'VE NEVER HEARD

is immune to the wiles of indwelling sin, but as Christians, we have an indwelling power that is entirely able to give us moment-by-moment victories. Whatever the number of days we have left, we need to embrace each of them in the same manner. We must not let the things of life—difficult or otherwise—get in the way. We are to begin each day anew.

A Necessary Transformation

Thy word I have treasured [hid] in my heart, that I may not sin against Thee.

Psalm 119:11

I urge you therefore, brethren, by the mercies of God, to present your bodies a living and holy sacrifice, acceptable to God, *which* is your spiritual service of worship. And do not be conformed to this world, but be transformed by the renewing of your mind, that you may prove what the will of God is, that which is good and acceptable and perfect.

Romans 12:1–2

But He answered and said, "It is written, 'MAN SHALL NOT LIVE ON BREAD ALONE, BUT ON EVERY WORD THAT PROCEEDS OUT OF THE MOUTH OF GOD.'"

Matthew 4:4

I repeat my belief that nothing has been more damaging to the witness of many in the church than the false idea of an eternal life guarantee. It has given people an utterly false sense of security and allowed them to drift away from Scripture almost entirely. All the survey data validates this to be true, and it is increasingly so as each day passes.

The vast majority of people's minds remain stuck in the morass of worldly and very human thought. Thus, the necessary transformation, which the above verses clearly reference, has never taken place. There is no question that a simple but genuine belief in Christ affirms a spiritual transformation, from spiritual death, or captivity, to spiritual life, freedom. But, it is only the Word of God—and a steady diet of it—that can transform the way a person thinks and, consequently, the way a person lives. And it must not be forgotten that it is the "living by faith" that affirms true discipleship.

We need to establish the importance of the Word of God in our lives. We simply cannot embrace the objective of holy living while continuing to ignore it. The things of life seem to demand our unwavering time and attention, but we should never allow ourselves to be managing such things to the exclusion of God's Word. We must find time for the embedding of Scripture deep within our hearts.

Toward the objective of holy living, there is nothing in life—for any person—that should transcend the importance of the Word of God and the influence of the Holy Spirit. There is no rule that establishes the frequency of our study of Scripture, i.e., hourly, daily, weekly, etc. However, the Scriptures are the essence of our interaction with the Lord; it is only by sincerely and frequently engaging that we afford ourselves our best chance of accomplishing that objective.

Set Your Mind on Things Above

> Set your mind on the things above, not on the things that are on earth. For you have died and your life is hidden with Christ in God. When Christ, who is our life, is revealed, then you also will be revealed with Him in glory.
>
> **Colossians 3:2–4**

> Whatever you do, do your work heartily, as for the Lord rather than for men; knowing that from the Lord you will receive the reward of the inheritance. It is Lord Christ whom you serve.
>
> **Colossians 3:23–24**

> Trust in the LORD with all your heart, and do not lean on your own understanding. In all your ways acknowledge Him, and He will make your paths straight.
>
> **Proverbs 3:5–6**

Typically, at some point each morning, we end up in front of a mirror. What we see in the initial moment is a reflection of ourselves. If we have truly died to self, as the Scripture calls us to do (see Matthew 10:39; Mark 8:35; John 12:25), we will embrace the eyes of the Lord in our eyes, and in that moment, for that day, set our minds on Him and the things above, not simply on whatever lies ahead.

It is not that we should avoid the things of the day (although avoidance may sometimes be the best decision); it is simply that we should endeavor to walk through the day in exactly the same way that Jesus would. It is possible because He is always present within us. And He is ready and willing to walk us through each and every day, to actually be our life if we will but learn to trust and rely on Him.

We need to get our heads around the idea that no matter where we are, no matter what we are doing, God wants us to be constantly serving and reflecting His Son. That can only be consistently possible as we endeavor to let His power direct and control our car. One day each of us will stand before the Son of God. In that moment, the account of our lives will have been recorded, and it will be unchangeable. By then, it will be too late to ask the Lord for a do-over.

Straight paths reflect holy living, and this is not something that just happens. We have to be intentional about purposing to take "every thought captive to the obedience of Christ" (2 Corinthians 10:5b). If we hope

THE GOSPEL YOU'VE NEVER HEARD

to be as Jesus was, obedient to His Father in all things, we have to develop a relationship with Him. Through the presence of His Spirit within us, we have free access to His mind and all that He is (see 1 Corinthians 2:16b). And we can know this for certain: He is waiting to meet with us in the pages of His book, and if we are willing to do His will, He will make His teachings known to us (see John 7:17). The greatest single error anyone can make in the living of life is to rely on his or her own thoughts and understanding. If we don't hide His word in our hearts, by default, that is exactly what happens.

A Rare Manner of Living

Do nothing from selfishness or empty conceit, but with humility of mind let each of you regard one another as more important than himself; do not *merely* look out for your own personal interests, but also for the interests of others.

Philippians 2:3–4

But prove yourselves doers of the word, and not merely hearers who delude themselves. For if anyone is a hearer of the word and not a doer, he is like a man who looks at his natural face in a mirror; for *once* he has looked at himself and gone away, he has immediately forgotten what kind of a person he was. But one who looks intently at the perfect law, the *law* of liberty, and abides by it, not having become a forgetful hearer but an effectual doer, this man shall be blessed in what he does.

James 1:22–25

The above Philippians verses define a manner of living that is entirely too rare in our world. Over the years, I have condensed the meaning of these verses into a simple maxim regarding the choice that every person makes. We choose one or the other:

Choice 1. Consider others as more important than myself.
Choice 2. There are no others; there is only me.

And what does our choice reveal?

Answer: we are slaves of the one whom we obey!

The verses from James put us back in front of the mirror again. If the face we are seeing is the Lord's, then the life we live will be a reflection of Him. Anything other than that means that the life we live is still our own. We will either have forgotten the law of liberty or not understood it. Jesus died to set us free, to give us the freedom to let Him be the Lord of our lives. Remember, the Scripture makes it plain that a person who claims to know Jesus, yet does not endeavor to keep His commandments, is a liar, and the truth is not in him (see 1 John 2:4).

Something Is Amiss in the World

> Finally, be strong in the Lord, and in the strength of His might. Put on the full armor of God, that you may be able to stand firm against the schemes of the devil. For our struggle is not against flesh and blood, but against the rulers, against the powers, against the world forces of this darkness, against the spiritual *forces* of wickedness in the heavenly *places.*
>
> **Ephesians 6:10–12**

> And not only this, but we also exult in our tribulations, knowing that tribulation brings about perseverance; and perseverance, proven character; and proven character, hope; and hope does not disappoint, because the love of God has been poured out within our hearts through the Holy Spirit who was given to us.
>
> **Romans 5:3–5**

The evidence that something is amiss in the world is undeniable. The arguments begin when we consider the cause of such a malady. In the true child of God, there should be no confusion, no wondering. We learn from the Scriptures that by the allowance of God, the whole of humanity exists in an environment dominated by spiritual warfare. It is warfare that reflects the big picture priority of God. God has provided a way for us to stand firm in the midst of the battle. We can do all things through Him who strengthens us (see Philippians 4:13). We have but to "dress" for that reality every day.

It is my conviction that, by and large, the world has failed to recognize the coming of Christ as a direct action of God. Why? Because the manner of living that the church has reflected has rarely evidenced the indwelling presence and life-altering power of Christ. Regrettably, that history is something that cannot be changed. But, it doesn't have to continue to be that way. The effectiveness of our lives as true children of God can be changed for the better if we will but recognize the why of His presence within us, and, in the light of that understanding, endeavor moment by moment to remain in and rely on Him.

Bart Erhman has stated that his agnosticism is a result of his "inability to understand how a good and loving God could be in control of this world given the miserable lives that most people—even believers— are forced to endure here."[1] What Mr. Erhman and so many others have failed to recognize is that God is not "in control" of this world. By His allowance, it is the evil one who is currently in charge (see 1 John 5:19b).

Even in the midst of the beauty and joy we can experience, we are daily surrounded by the ugliness, pain, inequities, and devastation of evil. And yes, it is by the hand of that evil force that "every five seconds a child dies of starvation in the world. Every five seconds."[2] But

THE GOSPEL YOU'VE NEVER HEARD

in the light of the gospel, we can know this for certain: because of the justness of God, not one of those innocent children (born into their circumstance through no fault of their own) has ever been nor will they ever be separated from the love and eternal presence of God.

Tribulation is in the world, and it is not a respecter of persons. It is only by the power of the Holy Spirit that we can endure and rise above the difficulties of life. How we deal with them, however devastating, reveals our true character and our bigger picture understanding. It should be His character that the world sees in us, not our own. And understand this: it is only as we reflect His character that our hope for eternity becomes validated as a hope that will not disappoint.

The Choice is Ours

That collection of verses is but a few of literally dozens of verses that speak to the manner in which true children of God should be endeavoring to live their lives. Based on Scripture, the true children of God are those who are being led by the spirit of God, not merely claiming possession of that Spirit (see Romans 8:14).

Every day the choice remains the same: will I drive my car myself, or will I let the Lord empower my hands? Will it be His will or mine? The Lord's presence in our car does not immunize us from sin, but it does offer a means of overcoming even the greatest of temptations, whatever they may be (see 1 Corinthians 10:13). Indeed, Jesus has not called us to an impossible task. He declares that He is even able to keep us from stumbling (see Jude 24).

Why is this possible? Because it is no longer the believer who lives for himself, but Christ who lives within him. The life that we each have will always be uniquely our own, but the manner in which we choose to live our lives should always be uniquely His.

There are no questions in life that a proper understanding of the gospel of the Son of God does not answer. And they are answers that have been available to us since He came into the world. It is only in Him that we can find the "pearl of great value" (Matthew 13:46), which is the understanding that has been missing from our lives (see 1 John 5:20).

In Christ, we can find the strength to overcome (see Philippians 4:13), assuming we have embraced that as our goal (see Revelation 21:7). And in Him, we find the truest reason for our being: life is but a very tiny moment in time, difficult as it might be, wherein we might gain eternity with God.

Each of us needs to ask ourselves:

Is that my hope?

If it isn't, it should be. Make it so!

THE GOSPEL YOU'VE NEVER HEARD

Deliberations

Questions for Reflection or Group Study

1. How do you react to the idea of living perfectly, i.e., in a manner that exactly reflects the holiness of God? Consider your day-to-day thought process. If it were scrolling across a publicly visible computer screen, what kind of dependency would it show?

2. What must happen for a person to be "transformed by the renewing of the mind"? What keeps you from spending more time in Scripture?

3. What is your experience of good versus evil in the world? Describe how your knowledge of Scripture has carried you through your most difficult times.

4. What is your reaction to the following: life is but a very tiny moment in time, difficult as it might be, wherein we might gain eternity with God? If that be true—and it is—how then should we live?

16

For Your Consideration

In his first letter to the church in Corinth, Paul wrote the following: "For the word of the cross is to those who are perishing foolishness, but to us who are being saved, it is the power of God" (1 Corinthians 1:18). He referred to Christ as the "power of God and the wisdom of God" (v. 24b) and declared that his message and his preaching "were not in persuasive words of wisdom, but in demonstration of the Spirit and of power, that your faith should not rest on the wisdom of men, but on the *power of God*" (vv. 4–5, emphasis mine). As Christians, do we think it reasonable to expect that a person whose faith is actually relying on the power of God should, in turn, be reflecting a manner of living that evidences such power?

Paul warned in his final letter to Timothy:

But realize this, that in the last days difficult times will come. For men will be lovers of self [...]

rather than lovers of God; [they will be] holding to a form of godliness, although they have denied its power; and avoid such men as these [...] [for they will be] always learning and never able to come to the knowledge [*epignosis*] of the truth.

2 Timothy 3:1–7

The Here and Now Reality

My writing acknowledges the above warning as a here and now reality. It has presented us with the *epignosis* of the truth, the "Washing Clothes" understanding of the gospel. It has made clear that Jesus did not sacrifice Himself to merely become a passenger in anyone's car. He gave His life in response to a plea from those who realized they were falling short, a plea from those who recognized they were being held as spiritual captives by a contrary power greater than their own.

Why are we Christians not realizing that today? Why are so many of us continuing to fall short? Why are so many living as though there were no power available to them at all? Because we have embraced an inaccurate gospel that denies its power!

The Lord said this: "And from everyone who has been given much, much shall be required" (Luke 12:48b). There is nothing of greater significance for any human being than the receiving of the Holy Spirit. But we must recognize it as an event that is not just about forgiveness and freedom; it is also about empowerment and obligation.

From John 1:12, we read: "But as many as received Him, to them He gave the right to become children of God, *even* to those who believe in His name." In Greek, the word for "right" is *exousia*, which can also mean "absolute power, authority."[1] Thus the above verse is better understood if read "to them He gave the power to *become* children of God" (emphasis mine).

Not Just His Presence Alone

The presence of the Lord in our car does not by itself make us children of God. But from a spiritual perspective, His presence most assuredly does make us completely free. There is no part of our human spirit that remains in any way attached to the sin presence that remains in our flesh. We are now entirely free to follow whomever we choose. The Scripture makes it clear that it is only those who are being led by the spirit of God that are truly the sons of God (see Romans 8:14).

Jesus is not sitting in our car, hoping that we will let Him drive every now and then. He is urging us to do for Him what He has already done for us. He is imploring us to die to self, to die for Him, to actually recognize that His way is the best and only way (see John 14:6a). He has already evidenced a personal power that is greater than the power of death (see Hebrews 2:14–15). And "for the joy that was set before Him" (Hebrews 12:2), He endured the cross in order to make *His power* available to us.

THE GOSPEL YOU'VE NEVER HEARD

But what we must understand about Jesus is that He will never arbitrarily remove our hands from the wheel. If we've accepted Him with the right understanding ("for apart from Me you can do nothing" [John 15:5b]), we should be willingly surrendering the wheel to Him in every moment of every day. We must recognize that this new Master/servant relationship is not like the old master/slave relationship. As regenerate Christians, we have been adopted as sons "by which we cry out, 'Abba! Father!'" (Romans 8:15b). Literally, picture the arms of a child reaching up: Dad to the rescue! He will not remove our hands, but He stands ready to empower them!

Jesus said that we must be working the works of the One by whom He was sent (see John 9:4a). That is why He came. That is what He is in our car to do. To work the works that were created beforehand, that we should walk in them (see Ephesians 2:10). That is precisely why Paul could so confidently declare, "I can do all things through Him who strengthens me" (Philippians 4:13).

What I Urge You to Consider

We have reached the end. Thank you for getting here, for staying the course. I have given you much to think about, much to contemplate. And by way of reminder, in the early part of this book, I accepted full responsibility for the things I would be writing, my confidence being in the One from whom I learned them. It remains my conviction that I have presented you with the core knowledge of the truth, the one foundation upon which all human beings should be living their lives (see 1 Corinthians 3:10–11).

237

By doing so, I want you to consider that I may have created a bit of a difficulty for you. There is a verse in Hebrews that reads: "For if we go on sinning willfully after receiving the knowledge of the truth, there no longer remains a sacrifice for sins" (10:26). That is a verse that was written of people who were sanctified (see v. 29). The only people in the history of life who have been sanctified are those who have accepted Christ. Is He in your car? If yes, then I ask you to prayerfully consider the following:

> Anyone who goes too far and does not abide in the teaching of Christ, does not have God; the one who abides in the teaching, he has both the Father and the Son. If anyone comes to you and does not bring this teaching, do not receive him into *your* house, and do not give him a greeting; for the one who gives him a greeting participates in his evil deeds.
>
> **2 John 9–10**

Indeed, I have given you much to consider. It is my sincerest hope that you will decide to make time to examine the Scriptures yourself, to "see whether these things [are] so" (see Acts 17:11b). "Now to Him who is able to keep you from stumbling, and to make you stand in the presence of His glory blameless with great joy [...] Amen" (Jude 24).

Endnotes

Introduction

1   Dallas Willard, The Divine Conspiracy (New York, NY: HarperCollins, 1997), xv.

2   Andy Crouch, "The Emergent Mystique," andy-crouch.com (blog), http://andy-crouch.com/articles/the_emergent_mystique.

3   Bob Smietana, "Americans Worry About Moral Decline, Can't Agree on Right and Wrong," Lifeway Research, May 9, 2017 https://lifewayresearch.com/2017/05/09/americans-worry-about-moral-decline-cant-agree-on-right-and-wrong.

4   Jackson Wu, "Why must we settle for part of the gospel?" Patheos, April 22, 2020, https://www.patheos.com/blogs/jacksonwu/2020/04/22/why-must-we-settle-for-part-gospel.

5   William F. Arndt and F. Wilbur Gingrich, Walter Bauer's A Greek English Lexicon of the New Testament (Chicago and London: The University of Chicago Press, 1979), 317.

Chapter 1

1   Sam Harris, Letter to a Christian Nation (New York: Vintage Books, a Division of Random House, Inc.,

2008), 106.

2   Christopher Hitchens, *god is not Great* (New York: Twelve, 2007), 122.

3   Bart D. Erhman, *Jesus, Interrupted* (New York: HarperOne, 2009), 275.

4   Ibid., 59.

5   Lillian Kwon, "Biblical Illiteracy in US at Crisis Point, Says Bible Expert," *The Christian Post*, June 16, 2014, http://www.christianpost.com/news/biblical-illiteracy-in-us-at-crisis-point-says-bible-expert-121626.

6   "Barna Studies the Research, Offers a Year-in-Review Perspective," Barna Group, December 20, 2009, https://www.barna.org/barna-update/faith-spirituality/325-barna-studies-the-research-offers-a-year-in-review-perspective.

7   George Gallup Jr. and Jim Castelli, "Americans and the Bible," Bible Review, June 1990, https://www.baslibrary.org/bible-review/6/3/18.

8   J. C. Ryle, Holiness (Grand Rapids, MI: Baker Book House, repr. 1883), 27-28.

9   Hitchens, 277.

Chapter 2

1   Sam Harris, *The End of Faith: Religion, Terror, and The Future of Reason* (New York: W. W. Norton & Company, Inc., 2004), 173.

2   Ibid., 73-74.

3   Bill Bright, "Four Spiritual Laws," Copyright 2007 Bright Media Foundation and Campus Crusade for Christ, https://campusministry.org/docs/tools/FourSpiritualLaws.pdf

Chapter 3

1 E. D. Hirsch, Jr., *Cultural Literacy* (Boston: Houghton Mifflin Company, 1987), 56–57.
2 Ibid., 40.
3 Ibid.

Chapter 4

1 Norman L. Geisler and Frank Turek, *I Don't Have Enough Faith to Be an Atheist* (Wheaton, IL: Crossway, 2004), 20.
2 Ibid.
3 Ibid.
4 Josh McDowell and Sean McDowell, *More Than a Carpenter* (Carol Stream, IL: Tyndale House Publishers, Inc., 1977, 2005, 2009), 1.
5 David Berlinski, *The Devil's Delusion: Atheism and Its Scientific Pretentions* (New York: Basic Books, 2009), 140.
6 Arndt and Gingrich, *A Greek-English Lexicon of the New Testament and Other Early Christian Literature* (The University Of Chicago Press: 1979) 639.
7 Sam Harris, *Letter to a Christian Nation* (New York: Vintage Books, a Division of Random House, Inc., 2008), 51.
8 Arndt and Gingrich, 664.
9 Virginia S. Thatcher, ed., *The New Webster Encyclopedic Dictionary of the English Language* (New York: Avenel Books, 1984), 316.

Chapter 5

1 Merriam-Webster, s.v. "unregenerate," accessed April 8, 2021, https://www.merriam-webster.com/dictionary/unregenerate.

Chapter 6

1   "What does retribution theology teach? Is it biblical?" Compelling Truth, accessed April 8, 2021, https://www.compellingtruth.org/retribution-theology.html.

2   J. B. Lightfoot, *Saint Paul's Epistle to the Colossians and to Philemon* (Grand Rapids, MI: Zondervan Publishing House, repr. 1879), 138.

3   Dave Hunt, *Beyond Seduction* (Eugene, OR: Harvest House Publishers, 1987), 5.

4   John R. W. Stott, *Men Made New: An Exposition of Romans 5-8* (Grand Rapids, MI: Baker Book House, 1984), 4.

5   Philip Schaff, *History of the Christian Church, Volume 1* (Peabody, MA: Hendrickson Publishers, Inc., repr. 2002), 766.

6   W. J. Conybeare and J. S. Howson, *The Life and Epistles of St. Paul* (Grand Rapids, MI: Wm. B. Eerdmans Publishing Company, repr. 1983), 28.

7   Grant R. Osborne, *Romans* (Downers Grove, IL: InterVarsity Press, USA, 2004), 44.

8   World Transformation Movement, accessed April 8, 2021, http://www.humancondition.com/the-human-condition.

9   Arndt and Gingrich, 183.

10 John Eidsmoe, *Historical and Theological Foundations of Law* (Powder Springs, GA: published jointly by American Vision Press and Tolle Lege Press, 2012), 249.

11 Ibid.

12 Torah: the law of God as revealed to Moses and recorded in the first five books of the Hebrew scriptures (the Pentateuch).

13 Sam Harris, *Letter to a Christian Nation* (New York:

THE GOSPEL YOU'VE NEVER HEARD

Vintage Books, a Division of Random House, Inc., 2008), 51.

Chapter 7
1 Robert Jewett, *Romans, A Commentary* (Minneapolis, MN: Augsburg Fortress Press, 2007), 434.
2 Ibid.

Chapter 8
1 Schaff, 766.
2 Osborne, 173.
3 Eidsmoe, 19.
4 Gary Hill, *The Discovery Bible* (Chicago, IL: Moody Press, 1987), 536.
5 Maurie Daigneau, *One Lord, One Truth, One Faith: The Only Legacy Worth Leaving* (iUniverse, Inc., 2004), 41.

Chapter 9
1 C. E. B. Cranfield, *Romans, A Shorter Commentary* (Grand Rapids, MI: William B. Eerdmans Publishing Company, 1985), 172.
2 Jewett, 484.
3 Arndt and Gingrich, 878.
4 Purpose Driven, accessed April 8, 2021, https://www.purposedriven.com/the-book.
1 Arndt and Gingrich, 598.
2 Ibid., 501.
3 Your Dictionary, s.v. "save," accessed April 8, 2021, https://www.yourdictionary.com/save.
4 The free Dictionary by Farlex, Inc., s.v. "save," accessed April 8, 2021, http://www.thefreedictionary.com/save.
5 Ibid.
6 Wikipedia, s.v. "Salvation," accessed April 8, 2021,

https://en.wikipedia.org/wiki/Salvation.

7   Spiros Zodhaites, *The Hebrew-Greek Key Word Study Bible* (Chattanooga, TN: AMG Publishers, 1990), 1704.

8   "Englishman's Greek: Chapter 8: the Greek Verb," the Middletown Bible Church, accessed April 8, 2021, http://www.middletownbiblechurch.org/egreek/egreek08.htm.

Chapter 12

1   J. B. Lightfoot, *Saint Paul's Epistles to the Colossians and to Philemon* (Grand Rapids, MI: Zondervan Publishing House, repr. 1879), 159.

2   A. T. Robertson, *Word Pictures in the New Testament, Volume IV* (Grand Rapids, MI: Baker Book house, copyright 1931), 480.

3   Hill, 537.

4   Ibid., 536.

5   Note: this references the first salvation because it is the only one that has occurred to this point and therefore appears in past tense, "saved."

6   Robertson, 77.

1   Stephen R. Covey, *The 7 Habits of Highly Effective People* (New York, NY: Free Press, 1989, 2004), 11.

2   Ibid., 99.

Chapter 13

1   "Newton's Laws - Lesson 4 - Newton's Third Law of Motion," The Physics Classroom, accessed April 8, 2021, https://www.physicsclassroom.com/class/newtlaws/Lesson-4/Newton-s-Third-Law.

2   Though not all agree that it is Satan in view in these passages (Ezek. 28:11–19 and Isa. 14: 12–19), it is my view.

Chapter 14

1 Bart D. Erhman, *God's Problem: How the Bible Fails to Answer Our Most Important Question—Why We Suffer* (New York: HarperOne, 2008), 189, 191.

2 Ibid., 48.

3 Jewett, 578.

Chapter 15

1 Bart D. Erhman, *Jesus, Interrupted: Revealing the Hidden Contradictions in the Bible (and Why We Don't Know About Them)* (New York: HarperOne, 2009), 273.

2 Erhman, *God's Problem*, 129.

Chapter 16

1 Arndt and Gingrich, 278.

About the Author

Maurie Daigneau is many things: a Christian, a husband, a father, a theologian, an entrepreneur, a former athlete, coach, and mentor. As a young man, he was the quarterback and co-captain of Northwestern University's football team, earning first team All-Big Ten honors during his senior year in 1971. He then went on to have a long and successful career as an entrepreneur, founding and running the pioneering athletic footwear company, Playmakers, Inc., and the national telecommunications firm, Affinity Corporation.

Along the way, Daigneau has lived an active life of faith. He earned an MS in theological studies from the Garrett-Evangelical Seminary in Evanston, Illinois. He was the Wisconsin State director of the Fellowship of Christian Athletes. He has also been a speaker and presenter at a variety of conferences, retreats, and events. Perhaps the greatest ongoing source of his faith experience is the weekly men's Bible study group that he has led and been a participant in for over thirty years.

He is the father of five and the grandfather of thirteen. He lives in Brookfield, Wisconsin with his wife of forty-eight years. You can read more about Maurie at www.mauriedaigneau.

CPSIA information can be obtained
at www.ICGtesting.com
Printed in the USA
BVHW040014011021
617866BV00016B/1240